To God Be the Glory

To God Be the Glory

The Story of My Life

Charles Farrell Crocker

LUCAS
PARK
BOOKS

ST. LOUIS, MISSOURI

ISBN: 978-1-60350-033-3

Published by Lucas Park books
www.lucasparkbooks.com

Printed in the United States of America

Contents

Contents

Acknowledgments

I am aware of the necessity of using the first person pronouns, I, my, and me, when writing a document such as this; however, it is an autobiography of my life. I remember a series of television programs which included a famous actor, Walter Brennan, who had a part in his lines to brag a lot in the stories. He would always follow his boasting with "no brag, just facts." It is my prayer that this story of my life will be read the same, "no brag, just facts."

I cannot make the story complete without some expressions of appreciation to some people who have played a big part in all I have said herein. First of all, I am thankful for my parents who encouraged me to use my talents to the glory of God.

My wife Mae has been a strong part of making the story what it is today and helping to make it all happen. At the time this story is being published, we have been married 63 years, and without her, I may not have gone into church work at all.

My children, David, Donna, and Judi, have been right there with me as I was preparing for this career. Their patience is greatly appreciated. As a part of seeing this autobiographical project through, they are covering the cost as a gift for my 80th birthday. A special word of thanks goes to Judi for putting all the material together, editing, and preparing it for publication.

It is my prayer that those who read this story will find enjoyment and, most of all, the encouragement to serve God in any possible way they can. That's what life is all about.

Charles Crocker
January 13, 2013

1

The Beginning

I was born in Glendale, South Carolina on May 2, 1932. Mom and Dad named me Charles Farrell Crocker. Charles came from my mother's oldest brother, Charlie Walker. Dad did not want me to be called Charles for fear that people would refer to me as Charlie. There was a famous bootlegger in Spartanburg County at the time I was born, and his name was Charlie Crocker. Anyway, Mama won that argument. It may be the only one she ever won. Farrell comes from Daddy's name; his middle name is Farrell. I have always been addressed as Charles. Very few people have ever addressed me as Charlie, not that I mind at all, but it just didn't happen very often.

I'm the youngest of four children born to my parents. There was Ellen Alberta Crocker, a sister; Earl, the oldest brother; and Dean; and then myself. Unfortunately, Ellen did not live. She was born a healthy baby, but Mama had such a difficult time giving birth. Forceps were used in those days, and this injured her in such a way that she did not live. She only lived for about 24 hours before she passed away.

I remember Dad telling the story, that with Ellen being the first child, he went down to the company store to pick up an item or two and the people in the store had already heard that the baby was born. They were teasing Dad, as people will do over the first child anyway. Dad started crying, and they wanted to know what was wrong. He told them she was born healthy but something happened as an injury in the birth, and she didn't make it. I've heard Mama say that when she felt of her little head, she could tell her skull was fractured in so many different places; it was just like jelly. I've always thought that if she had lived, she would have been an invalid all of her life.

Ellen was buried in the cemetery next to our house, in Uncle Charlie's plot. In those days, they didn't make a big to-do over a child like that, and she was buried in a very small grave right next to Uncle Charlie's grave. Every time I went to that grave I saw the field rock they put there for a headstone. There was no writing on it of course, but it was there just to mark where the grave was. That stone is no longer there, but I know where the grave is. It's about fifty yards from the Crocker plot. The Crocker plot can be seen inside a wrought iron fence in the edge of that cemetery. That's where my great-grandparents were buried, my grandparents, Uncle Elmond, and other Crockers. Uncle Elmond was my dad's brother who was killed at age 27. I'll say more about him later.

Mama undoubtedly had a very difficult time giving birth to children, taking into account what happened with Ellen, and she almost died when I was born. I was an unusually large baby. I weighed 10 pounds and 5 ounces. I was actually a month old when I was born. My mother carried me for 10 months. I remember my mother saying that she was not supposed to get pregnant again. The doctor had cautioned her because of the difficult time she had with Ellen, that she should not get pregnant again. She did, and almost died when I was born.

The cemetery I've already mentioned is very much a part of my life story because of where we lived, being so close to it. The day I was born, there was another Crocker that was just a year or two old, named George. He was the son of Uncle Albert and Aunt Ella. He drowned in a tub of water. I never knew the details of that, but the child was able to get to the tub somehow, and it was full of water, and he drowned. The people who attended the funeral for that baby were friends of Uncle Albert and Aunt Ella. It was so convenient for them to come right back through our house after the burial since our house was at the edge of the cemetery. The people came through the house to see the new baby. Mama was still in bed of course, after giving birth that day and having nearly died. She said that my eyes followed the people coming by the bed, just like a month-old baby would. I always thought that was very interesting. I remember Mama saying the doctor would not let her go to sleep, that if she went to sleep, she probably wouldn't awaken.

When I was about six months old, we moved to Rock Hill, South Carolina. I never did quite know why we moved to Rock Hill, but I'm assuming it had to do with Dad's work. Dad was selling insurance at that time, with Liberty Life Insurance Company, and I think he was transferred to Rock Hill. However, this was right at the edge of the Great Depression, and people were not buying insurance. They couldn't see buying insurance so they could be put away right when they died if they couldn't put food on the table. That was a very difficult time. I've heard Mama say that many times she watered down the milk we drank so we would have enough. I'm sure it wasn't watered down much, but it had to be stretched as far as possible.

Dad went on to Rock Hill ahead of us to find a place to live and do some necessary things for our coming later. He found a house, or maybe part of a house for rent on Saluda Street in Rock Hill. The house is no longer there, but it was on the right side of Saluda Street, down from Black Street about a quarter of a mile.

Almost immediately, Daddy became a choir director at White Street Baptist Church. He went to that church when he was in Rock Hill by himself. He attended choir practice on Wednesday night. Mr. H. L. Shaw was directing the choir at that time, and when he found out that Daddy had been directing the choir at Glendale Baptist Church, he felt like he was only a fill-in so he asked Daddy to come on up and take over the rehearsal. I always thought that was kind of funny, that Daddy would do that, not having any idea what they were singing or having any time to prepare. I compare that to when I had to prepare for a choir rehearsal I had in Asheville.

When the rest of the family first went to Rock Hill, I was a babe in arms, about six months old. We attended White Street Baptist Church, named for its location on White Street in the town of Rock Hill. On our first Sunday at the church, the pastor introduced Mama to the church. He said "She is sitting on such-and-such-a pew, with a recent gift from heaven in her arms." That recent gift from heaven, I want you to know, was me.

Interestingly enough, there's another thing that people probably don't know. Dad played the organ on occasion for worship services at Glendale Baptist before going to Rock Hill. It was a pump organ of course, and the first time Mama saw him, he was leaving the choir loft because the organist hadn't shown up (I don't know if it was bad weather, or what it was that caused the organist not to show up). Dad left the back row of the choir loft and went down and finished the service playing the organ. Daddy had already noticed Mama; she was a visitor. He was going to try to find out who that beautiful woman was back there at a certain place. He did, and it was love at first sight.

That rehearsal at White Street Baptist Church is how Daddy met Mr. H. L. Shaw, who became his friend, and the Shaw family and our family were very close from then on. Mr. Shaw helped Dad get a job at the Aragon Mill. Since he had worked at Glendale Mill, he knew how to do certain things that would enable him to get a job right away. He served as a loom fixer and a weaver.

A very interesting part of our life in Rock Hill was soon after we moved there. We needed to have a house on the Aragon Mill village. There was not one available. Mr. and Mrs. Shaw offered for us to come and live with them until a house came open. Textile mills in the South furnished houses for the employees to have a place to live. They were charged a very small amount for rent. I recall Dad saying that for the houses we lived in at first, the mill would take the rent out of his paycheck. He paid fifty cents a room per week. So most of the time our house was four large rooms, and of course, this was two dollars rent. You've gotta remember this was during the Depression, and money was scarce.

The Shaws opened their doors to us, and we moved in. I don't know how or where we stored furniture; I know there wouldn't have been enough room in the Shaw's house to store furniture. That's another thing I never thought to ask Mama and Daddy, "What happened to our furniture while we were living with the Shaws?"

The Shaw family at that time was composed of Mr. and Mrs. Shaw and their sons Lloyd, Howard, Marson, Gene, and Jack. Jack was the same age that I was; our birthdays were about three months apart. We were both sleeping together in the same baby bed. For that reason, and many other reasons, Jack and I became very close friends throughout the rest of his life. (He died a few years ago in Columbia.) In addition to the names I've given of the Shaw family, Paul and Phyllis came later, and there were five of us Crockers. How we lived in a four-room house, I will never understand. It could have been a five-room house; I don't recall exactly where the Shaws lived. Some of the houses had five rooms. I don't know how we did it. Dean asked Howard Shaw one time, "How long did we live with you all down on Kuykendall Street?" Howard said, "Too long!"

When Dad asked Mr. Shaw how he wanted to work the grocery bill, and other expenses, Mr. Shaw said, "If your wife will do the cooking, and if you will pay the amount for the groceries needed for your family, that's all the pay I need." My mother was a wonderful cook. She was very good at using leftovers, although we didn't have many leftovers. She could put stuff together and add a little of this, a little of that, and make the most out of the smallest amount of food you've ever seen. Mr. Shaw swore that during that time his grocery bill was *less* than it was to start with. He wanted this arrangement so his wife could work in the mill, which she needed very much to do.

A short while later, probably a few months after we moved in with the Shaw family, a house came open. It was on the lower end of Frayser Street, there on the village. Living there was the first knowledge I have of being alive in this world. I was approximately three years old when we moved. There were some interesting and very unusual things that happened while we were there, and that's why I remember them. People say, "You just remember us talking about it," but that's not so. I distinctly remember the things I'm about to tell you.

Dean and Earl made a tent out of tow sacks and some equipment they got out of the scrap pile at the mills. It was put together in a back alley behind the house. When I was in the tent and stood up, my head was pressing a little against the top of the tent, and Wallace Moon, who lived up behind us, reached over with a stick or something and tapped me on the head, and I started crying. He and Earl got in a fight over it. Earl didn't like anybody messing with his baby brother!

I also would go next door to where the Beckhams lived, and sometimes it would be a meal time. They were amused at how I liked cabbage, being such a young age. I would eat cabbage or most anything else they'd put in front of me. I know I had plenty to eat at home, but I just enjoyed eating, and still do. The McGinnis house was close by too. They had large fig trees in the back yard. I recall eating figs from those trees.

Dad organized the Majestic Quartet, which did most of their rehearsing at our house on Frayser Street. This quartet was composed of Daddy as first tenor, Gilliam Lowery as second tenor, H. L. Shaw as baritone, and Will Lowery as bass. At that time, Dad had a guitar and a violin in addition to George Finley playing the piano. Fletcher Talley and his sister played the violin and the guitar.

Even at a very young age, I was fascinated by those instruments. I remember picking up my spoon at the dinner table, pretending it was a guitar. I held it like it was a guitar, and strummed that spoon. Mama got a kick out of that. Even at an early age, I realized, and they realized, that a musical interest was brewing in me. Mama would say, "Looky there, he's keeping perfect time with the music" when we were listening to the radio.

I remember a story Earl told me after I became a grown man, a story I'd never heard before. It was Christmastime and also right in the middle of the Great Depression. I was about three years old at the time, so this took place on Christmas Eve, about 1935.

Christmas was always big at our house. We never had a lot of money to spend on Christmas, especially my Dad during the Depression. But we were always glad to have each other, and we were able to enjoy Christmas with Mama's good cooking and sitting around the old coal heater, telling stories. Most of the stories came from Daddy, and we enjoyed hearing him talk about things he did when he was a boy.

On this particular Christmas Eve, it was late enough in the evening that we had all gone to bed. Earl, being the oldest, was awake. Dean and I were asleep, and I don't remember hearing this, but Earl told how Mama asked Daddy if he was able to find anything they could afford to give us for Christmas. Daddy said, "I looked and looked, and I didn't have the money to do anything; I wasn't able to get anything." While he was talking, he began crying. Daddy was not a person to cry very easily, but at a time like that, he was very sad, and he and Mama both were crying. She started crying because he was crying. They were both thinking about us. We were in the same room they were in, all three of us children sleeping in the same bed.

I don't know what time this took place, but it was late enough that we certainly were not expecting anybody to come see us. We were already in bed. All of a sudden, there was a knock at the door. Mama said, "I wonder who in the world that could be?" Daddy said, "I don't know, but I'll go see." He got up and slipped his bathrobe on and went to the door. It was his sister, Venice, and her husband Roy. They were never able to have children, and we became just like their children to them. I never knew anyone who enjoyed Christmas any more than Aunt Venice. She always enjoyed having a big meal with all the family there. She would set the table days in advance, cooking to get ready for it.

Daddy opened the door and saw who it was. He said, "What on earth are y'all doing here? Come in!" They not only brought themselves in, but they brought a lot of gifts for us children. I don't remember, but I think there was something there for Mama and Daddy too. I don't know how they knew that we were not getting anything for Christmas, but they may have just assumed it because of the way the economy was during the Great Depression. They knew that if we got something from "Santa Claus" it wouldn't be much, and they wanted to help make Christmas special for us boys.

As I think back on these earliest years of my life, I can see how the Lord had a hand in our family's move to Rock Hill and in bringing other people into our lives that would later become friends who meant a great deal to us throughout our lives. Even though it was a difficult time during the Depression, we had a loving family, a good home, a church, and close friends, for which we were very thankful.

Carrie and Farrell Crocker

Charles at about six months

2

112 Long Street

After we lived there on Frayser Street for a while, another house came open at 112 Long Street. The rooms were bigger, and we would have a little more room, so Daddy accepted the house.

One of the funniest things that happened in my early life was this little story. Mama and I had gone down to 112 Long Street, and she was going to do some cleaning to get things ready for us to move down to that place. It was in the wintertime, and we were gone long enough that the fire in the heater back up on Frayser Street had gone out, and, I guess, cooled down. It was just a little laundry heater back in the kitchen area; it wasn't hooked to any water pipes, but it was a way for us to stay warm. A bird had gone down the chimney (it wasn't a chimney swift, but an English sparrow) and worked his way out through the stove pipe and down in the heater, amongst all those ashes. When we returned home, Mama immediately opened up the heater with stove lifters to lift the plates out in order to build a fire in that heater. That bird flew out and got dust all over us. It scared Mama half to death. I laughed and laughed and laughed about that bird!

At first, we were still members at White Street Baptist Church. We had gone back over there for a special program that they called the Christmas Tree. Churches in those days would have a large Christmas tree and bring presents especially for the children. They would call them up to the front to get their gifts. We had gone back to White Street for that occasion, and there was a little pop gun that Dad and Mama had bought and put under the tree for me. It was a little gun that you cocked and put a cork in the end of the barrel. It was fastened to a string, and when you fired the cork it would go out a foot or two from the barrel, but that was close enough to me that it hit my arm and I started crying. I remember that so well. By this time we were living at 112 Long Street. I was about three and a half or four years old at the time.

Sometime after we moved to Long Street, I had my first very serious illness. I had double pneumonia, meaning that both lungs were infected. I was a very sick boy. Doctor Simpson was practicing medicine in Rock Hill at that time, and he was coming to the house to see me. In those days, doctors would come to the house to treat patients. After Dr. Simpson had seen me several times, he told Mama and Daddy that he had done all he could do, and that I may not make it. But he followed that by saying "I also have a new young doctor just out of med school in with me, and he knows a lot more new things to treat such as Charles has. I'd like for him to come in and see Charles." Mama and Daddy said, "Anything you say, we'll try." They really thought I was goner.

Dr. Bundy was this new young doctor that Dr. Simpson mentioned. He came to see me. He told Mama something to do that was very, very strange to her, but I can understand now why he said what he did. He told Mama to build up a fire in the fireplace (which was the way we heated that room), just as big a fire as she could get, and open every window in the room. It was in the cold part of the wintertime, and it seemed kind of funny. As I thought about it later, what he was doing was trying to get oxygen in that room. We didn't have oxygen tents or any way of administering oxygen to a person. The fire was burning up so much of the oxygen it was making matters worse as far as pneumonia was concerned.

Dr. Bundy left, and Mama built up the fire—it was roaring—and opened the windows, and there was a door in that room that went out on the porch. She opened the door too. I don't know what kind of medicine they gave me, if any at all, but when Dr. Bundy came back the next time, he said, "according to my calendar, he's going to go through a crisis, probably tonight, and tomorrow he'll either be with us or he'll be gone." That scared Mama and Daddy to death. Mama said that the next day, when Dr. Bundy came in, he was handing Mama his coat and hat and didn't even look at her. He was looking straight over toward the bed at me, and immediately a big ol' smile appeared on his face. He said, "He has passed the crisis; I think he's going to make it."

That illness put a scar on my lung, and it shows up every time I have an x-ray of my lungs. Just recently, I went, at the doctor's request, to a pulmonary doctor to have my lungs checked out because of serious illness I've had recently. He wanted to make sure my lungs were okay. That scar showed up on those pictures, and they called me about it. I told them, "That's been on my lung for more than 70 years."

I got the royal treatment when I was sick—not that I enjoyed being sick—but I recall our neighbor across the street, a Mrs. Dendy, was making homemade ice cream, and she brought a great big dish of ice cream over to me. I thought that was the best thing I'd ever put in my mouth! Probably, it was the first time I'd had any ice cream, and being homemade at that, it was really, really good.

We had a lady named Mrs. Hawkins who delivered milk to us. She had several cows and lived out in the country. We got buttermilk and butter from her. When I was recuperating from my pneumonia, she brought some sweet milk. I'd not had sweet milk up to that time, because Mama had buttermilk that we could drink, and she would use it to make bread. A couple of times when Mrs. Hawkins came to bring our milk she brought me some sweet milk. The next time she came, she didn't bring any sweet milk. I asked Mama, "Did Mrs. Hawkins' sweet milk cow gone dry?" That was one of the stories Mama told all the time she was alive; it tickled her so.

Sometime after that episode with pneumonia, Dean was ill. The pastor came to see him, and he said, "Dean, what do you want to do when you grow up?" Dean said, "Well, I guess I'm gonna be a preacher." And he looked at me and said, "Charles, what are you going to do?" I said, "I'm gon' h'moke!" [smoke] I was too young to really know what I was saying.

Not too awfully long after we moved down on Long Street, I had a sweetheart. Her name was Dotsy Ruth. I never did know whether her first name was Dotsy and the last name was Ruth. It doesn't matter. We called her Dotsy Ruth. We played together really often out in the back alley that went down behind the houses, where the garbage can was and where the outhouses were. Everybody at the Aragon Mill village had an outhouse. We did not have indoor plumbing until I was a teenager. Our water supply was one faucet on the back porch, coming up from the ground, and that was it.

Dotsy and I played in the back alley because she lived on the street one block over, and the back of their house faced the back of our house. So the back alley was the place we met to play. I had a very narrow escape there when either the mill company or the city, I don't recall which, (that part of the village was in the city, and it may have been the city) was putting up new telephone posts up and down the back alley, then ran current and electricity to the houses from there. They had dug new holes and taken up the old poles, and they hadn't filled the holes. Dotsy and I were sitting at the top of one of the holes, with our feet dangling down in the hole. It had rained the night before, and the loose dirt that was left in the hole became a soupy, soggy mess.

We were throwing little clods of dirt, rocks, or whatever we could pick up, dropping them down in the hole. It made a kind of design, splattering in that mud. It was fascinating. But the thing was, I got too close to the edge of the hole, and I slid off in there. Well, there was enough of that soupy mess down in that hole that my feet got stuck. There was no way I could get out of that hole. The telephone post hole was about five or six feet deep, and I was only about four or four and a half years old at that time, and not a big boy at all. I remember trying to reach for any little clod sticking out on the side of that hole to help me crawl out, but there wasn't any need in trying it. I just couldn't get out.

Dotsy decided she'd better go and tell somebody. Instead of going to tell my mother that I was in that hole, she went to her mother. Her mother didn't know about the hole, and she assumed that Dotsy was talking about the toilet hole. Dotsy's mother came across the back alley to our house and got Mama out to the back and said, "Mrs. Crocker, Charles has fallen into the toilet hole." So Mama and Ms. Ruth were running up and down the back alley looking in all the toilets. They could hear me calling out, "Mama! Mama! Mama!" They didn't know about the other hole; didn't even know it was there.

All of a sudden, Mama looked and saw the dirt piled up that had been in that hole, and she ran over and looked down, and there I was. I'll never forget the look on her face, nor the way I felt. The top of that round hole formed a frame for her face. She was one more beautiful sight! Mama would have pulled me out or pulled me in two, one or the other, because she was really strong. I have used that story many times, talking to children at choir camps and other places about the fact that God will pull us out of the miry clay if we will let him and trust in him.

I remember becoming fascinated with matches. Matches were used more in those days for lighting the oil stove and building a fire in the stove to keep warm. There was some smoking going on too, so matches were used an awful lot. Dotsy Ruth and I, when the grass was dead in the wintertime, would set fire to the grass and let it burn just a little, then put it out. It's a wonder we didn't cause something dangerous or get burned. That was one of the things I remember doing.

I also had a playmate named Ben Curtis. Ben lived in the house on the very end of the street, on the right. They had in their yard, next to the sidewalk, large smelling oranges. These were about the size of golf balls. They were not edible, and had a kind of bitter smell. We took his wagon and would pretend we were gathering oranges, taking them to sell them and so forth.

Ben and I also did something we shouldn't have done. A neighbor down the street just a little ways asked Ben and me to go down to the flat. The flat was where the hill came down from the Aragon and from town and there was an area at the bottom of those hills called the flat. It was flat for just a few hundred yards. There was a café, pool hall, barber shop—a typical kind of place between mill village and town. She gave us a little bit of money to go down and get her a popsicle. She didn't give us enough money to get one for ourselves, she just wanted us to do her a favor.

Well, Ben and I went down, and we bought the popsicle—one of those sherbet kind with two sticks. We started back toward the house, and it was too tempting—you know what I'm about to tell! "She won't mind if we take a little bite off one of these." We each took a bite, and it tasted so good, we took another bite. When we got back to her house, half that popsicle was gone. She got mad. Why she didn't give us enough money to buy us one, I don't know. I wondered why she never did ask us again to go get her a popsicle, but I think I've figured it out.

Living right next door to Ben Curtis was Earl Burgess, who also worked at the Aragon Mill. He had a mill house like the one we lived in. They had a daughter who was born with what they called a water head. Her head was very, very large, and the rest of her body was not so large. She was an invalid; she could not walk on her own. She lived in a wheelchair. Her mother would bring her out—the house didn't have steps, so there was a way to get the wheelchair in and out of the house.

Ben and I would play with her and entertain her. She was a really sweet girl, but she was very sensitive about her condition. We were just very small children, and we would make the mistake of asking her about it. When we did, she would start crying. We played like we were cooking. They had some flowers along the walkway. The flowers had seed, and we played like we were in the garden, gathering those seeds, pretending they were edible, and so forth. She would take those and pretend to mash them up, making something edible out of it. We had a good time playing with her and didn't realize we were doing something good. Being so young ourselves, we didn't realize this was something we should do when we grew up, to help others.

Living next door to us on Long Street was a family named Blackwell. They had several daughters in the family and one boy named Albert. He was very, very cross-eyed. He had other problems and was sent to school where he could get the training he needed to cope with his physical problems.

But I'm going to confess something that I did that I'm not proud of, and I don't know why in the world I did it. One of those girls was in the yard, and I guess I had heard the term "son of a bitch" somewhere. I looked at her and said, "you son of a bitch." I didn't even know what I had said, or where I had heard it. She said, "Oh Charles, you shouldn't say that!" I don't think Mama or Daddy ever knew I did that; no one told on me, but that was one thing I never could understand—why I thought of that phrase and why I did it.

The Blackwells kept little pigs under their house until they were big enough to take them over to the pasture where a lot of mill people had pigs, cows, and so forth. You could rent a cow barn, and a lot of people milked cows, furnishing milk for the family, just like they did back in the old, old days, and like those people did when they lived on a farm.

I had a conversation one day with my mother about my age. I remember we were walking up the sidewalk to visit the Shaws, who lived about a block away, and I asked Mama how old I was. She said, "You're five years old." About a day later, I asked her again, and she said, "Well, you're still five years old." That happened two or three times. I said, "I won't ever be anything but five years old! Five years old!" She laughed and told that on me until the day she died. Now I'm eighty years old. Eighty years old! That's a lot of difference!

To show you how young children look at things sometimes, I remember hearing boys on the mill village use all kinds of language. Mama would hear some of it, and she would tell us boys, "Don't ever talk like that! Don't ever use those words!" They were saying things like "God a'mighty" and Mama would say, "That's so bad! Don't ever use that."

Now, I'm as truthful as I can be. We would go to church on Sunday, and in the morning service many times we would sing "Holy! Holy! Holy! Lord God Almighty!" and I could not understand—if it was bad to say that out on the street and out in the village, why was it not bad at church? Certainly you shouldn't use that kind of language at church! But that was a small boy thinking.

Earl had a wagon that he'd had for years. He probably brought it to Rock Hill from Glendale, where we were living when I was born. The wagon had some age on it, and the way the wheels fastened on the wagon, instead of having the right thing, called the cotter pin, to hold the wheel on the wagon, he had a nail stuck in there and bent. When he scooted the wagon, you'd put your right knee in the wagon and hold the tongue of the wagon in your right hand, and your left foot would scoot the wagon, just like a scooter. Dean had a scooter one time.

We went barefooted an awful lot in the summer time, of course. As soon as it got warm enough, we'd throw our shoes off and go barefooted. Earl was barefooted and scooting his wagon along. That nail stuck in the end of the axle to hold the wheel on was bent so it would stay in there, but the point of the nail was sticking out. He hit it with his ankle and stuck that nail nearly through his left ankle. I remember how he cried!

When we got a little older, we had ST37, which was an antiseptic that would kill germs and what-have-you, but back in those days, you'd just put kerosene on it. Yes, I said kerosene. There seemed to be a healing power that kerosene had, and it was used quite a bit like that.

There was another wagon on the village that was owned by Ray Revells. He was the Super's boy. The superintendent of the mill (they called him the Super) was Mr. Revells, and his son Ray had a very, very fine wagon. It made all the boys on the village envious. Each of the four wheels had balloon tires that you put air in, instead of solid tires like were on Earl's wagon. They had a valve just like an automobile tire. That wagon was also equipped with ball bearings that would have a whole lot less friction, and it would go down a hill really fast.

Earl talked to Ray about letting him ride down Long Street in that wagon. Long Street was a long hill. We had sidewalks and curbs, but the road itself was dirt. Some of us were standing out in front of the house, and Dad was standing out there talking to a friend. Earl pulled that wagon to the top of that hill and got in it and started down. That thing would go twice as fast as Earl's wagon because of the way the wheels were made. When he got down in front of the house, he lost control of it and ran into the tree. Knocked him cold as a milkshake. Of course, Daddy ran over and picked him up and began to see if he could bring him back. When he came to, he started crying. Daddy took him in the house and patched him up.

Well, Earl didn't ask Ray if he could ride in that wagon anymore. He was satisfied with his old one that wouldn't go so fast. (By the way, Earl was about 11 years old, because he was six years older than I.)

Another kid close by had a pedal car. I thought that was the greatest thing I had ever seen. I would have been the happiest boy in the world if I could have had a pedal car. It actually had pedals and you could ride in the thing and work the pedals back and forth; it would go down the sidewalk. I would lie in bed at night and dream about having a pedal car, except in my dream (it was a made up dream; I wasn't asleep), mine actually had a motor in it. I would pretend I was riding over the mill village there. I had a crush on a girl that was more of a young teenager, and I thought she was the prettiest thing I'd ever seen. Her name was Betty Ford. In my dreaming, I dreamed she would ride in that little car with me. I don't know how we both would have gotten in it, but she was riding in it with me. I was taking her all over the mill village.

Another thing that was interesting about living at 112 Long Street was that for a while we had boarders. We had a man who lived with us for a while named John Wallace. I don't remember how long he lived with us. He was not a relative, but he paid board [paid for his meals], and it helped out with expenses during the Depression. But later on, we had several ladies that boarded with us. You've got to remember this was a four-room house. It seemed like the rooms were large back then, but as I go in one of those houses now and look at it, they're not all that large. Mama and Daddy slept in the front bedroom and gave those ladies the back bedroom. They were being transferred over there from a mill in Greenville, South Carolina.

These were my young boyhood years, before I started to school. We did not have fancy toys, but had good clean fun because life was simple there on the mill village. I enjoyed those days and had good times with my young playmates.

3

41 Community Street

Dad had an agreement with the mill company that if keeping the boarders didn't work out, we could have our choice of whatever house was available on the village. Earl, Dean, and I agreed that was one of the worst stretches of time that we remember growing up. It was not a satisfactory arrangement with three boys still at home and the boarders living with us. It wasn't a pleasant thing at all.

Even though we moved to a new, much larger house at 41 Community Street in August of 1938, we continued to take in boarders. In this new house there was more room, but it still was hard on us three boys. There were times when we had to be so quiet when one of them was ill.

One of the ladies who boarded with us was named Bessie Allen. She was becoming the cloth room overseer at the Aragon Mill. This made her eligible for her own place, a much larger house just across the street from the mill. It had three large bedrooms, a living room, kitchen, and a room called a "sleeper" on the back of the house. The sleeper was a room used by people who worked on the third shift because it was cooler. There were windows about halfway down on three sides of the room.

Bessie Allen had a bad heart, and she was ill quite a bit, so we had to be very quiet all the time. Mama would give us wieners and some hot dog buns, and we'd go over to the cow pasture and have us a wiener roast just to get away. It certainly wasn't that these people were not nice; they were good people, but the arrangement of living all together just was not good. Mama did the cooking for the whole bunch.

I was six years old on May 2 before we moved to the new house, and I was ready to start to school at Northside Grammar School. Earl was a seventh grader when I started to school, and he was the one who took me to school for the first time to have my eyes checked and other necessary things like that which they had everybody do. Dean was in the fourth grade at that time. We called it grammar school back in those days, and now they call it elementary.

Dean did a funny thing when he started to school. (We were living on Long Street at that time.) Mama took him to school, and on the way back to the house, she stopped to talk to a friend, Mrs. Hawkins. When she got home, Dean was on the porch swing at the front of the house. She said, "Dean, what in the world are you doing here?" He said, "They expect me to stay over there all day without a drink of water! I came home to get me some water!" Of course, he didn't waste any time getting out of that porch swing, getting him some water, and getting back to school!

Earl was in the seventh grade at Northside, and that was the last grade of elementary school. There were no middle schools back in those days. At that time, eighth grade began high school and there were only four grades in high school. The eleventh grade was the last grade. Earl brought his report card home, the first one in the seventh grade, and he had made straight E's. A grade of "E" in those days was the same as an A today. They used E's for Excellence instead of using A's as we have most of the time since then. Daddy told Earl if he would make straight E's the rest of the year like on that first report card he would buy him a new bicycle so he could ride a bicycle to high school in the eighth grade. Earl agreed and made straight E's the whole year in the seventh grade.

Dad kept his promise, although he didn't have a lot of money. He bought the bicycle on an installment plan, and it took him a while to pay for it. We knew the day Daddy left the house to go to town to buy Earl a bicycle. They knew what kind they wanted, and Dad went by himself. Earl was so anxious—we all were—to see that new bicycle. We were looking down one direction, where we would normally look to see people coming from town and weren't looking the other way. I happened to look the other way, and Dad was coming around the corner, riding the bicycle. It was a Schwinn Excelsior, which was one of the best bicycles you could buy in those days. We later fell in love with the Columbia bicycle because that was the one sold at White's Bicycle Shop in town.

Earl almost immediately got him a paper route, delivering the *Charlotte News* on the mill village and a few other places. He used the bicycle to deliver the papers. He enjoyed having a little money in his pocket too.

I remember December 7, when the Japanese bombed Pearl Harbor. The person who brought the *Charlotte News* to Rock Hill brought Earl some papers by for us to sell as "extras". We'd go down the street yelling, "Extra! Extra! Read all about it! Jap planes bomb Pearl Harbor!" I hardly knew what I was saying, but Earl coached me on it and told me exactly what to say, and we were peddling the newspaper. The paper route put about six or seven dollars a week in Earl's pocket, which in those days, was a good bit of money.

He wanted a BB gun, which he bought. It was a Daisy Carbine, a very powerful BB gun, which was the forerunner of the Daisy Red Ryder Carbine. That was also the beginning of my learning to shoot a rifle, which came in handy one day.

Our next door neighbor had some boot-legged chickens. They were kind of a dark color, had feathers all the way down their feet, and were funny looking birds. Those bantam chickens would get in Mama's salad patch out in the back. We'd scare those things out, and the next thing we knew, they'd be right back in there. Scare them out, they'd be right back in there.

Another time they got in there, and I said, "Mama, those chickens are in the salad patch." She said, "Well go scare 'em out." I said, "Mama, can I shoot 'em?" She said, "Go right ahead!" I took Earl's high powered BB gun, went out there and propped on the side of the house and aimed really good, shot and killed one of those chickens, dead as a doornail! I went back in the house, set the gun in the corner, and said, "Well, I pinked him off!" Mama laughed about that the rest of her life, about how a third grader came in with a rifle and said "I pinked him off."

I used Earl's rifle because my little single shot BB gun wasn't powerful enough to shoot that far. I would put the BB's in my mouth and spit them down the barrel one at a time to shoot them. It's a wonder I didn't get strangled or something! That may be what's wrong with my stomach today; I may have swallowed a few of them!

I remember one time when I was at home. I don't recall why I wasn't in school. We shot those old nasty sparrows that built nests around the house. Mites would get in the house because of those sparrows. We were death on those sparrows. I had my little single shot out there, and one of the birds lit on a water cut-off on the house next door. I got a really lucky shot and killed that bird. I picked it up and took it back to the house.

I showed it to a black lady that was helping Mama some with washing and ironing. She said, "Poor little bird! I don't see how you could shoot a poor little bird like that." That got me to crying, and I was sorry I had shot it then. I really did it up right—there was a small shoe box at the house that I put the bird in, and I dug a hole out in the back, and buried it.

The funny thing was, when Dean and Earl came home, I told them about it.

Earl said, "Aw, you didn't hit that bird!" I said, "Yes, I did!"

"Aw, you can't shoot well enough to hit a little ol' bird at that distance!"

"Well I know I did!"

"No, you didn't do that!" Dean joined in on it.

I got mad and went out, dug it up and showed it to them! Those were the good ol' days. But at least they believed me when I showed it to them.

The house we were living in was right across the road from the mill where Daddy worked. The boarder I have already mentioned, named Bessie Allen, had a business agreement with me to carry "Peggy" out to the outhouse (to the toilet) every day, and she would pay me 10 cents a week. Remember that we did not have indoor toilets. When we were living there, we did have a bathtub and lavatory in a room we called the bathroom, but we did not have a commode. She would pay me to carry her slop jar out and empty it in the toilet, which I did faithfully.

I saved my money, and that's what I used to buy that single-shot rifle. I saved enough money to buy me a big red wagon. It was big to me; it was a full-sized wagon, with a tongue on it, rounded on the front end, which made it really nice for guiding it with the tongue while I was scooting it along with my left foot. That wagon cost $2.98. I bought it at Rock Hill Hardware. The same wagon today would probably cost $25 or $30 at least.

Another interesting thing that happened while we were living there was my cutting some kindling to build a fire. We heated with a coal heater, and we had to have kindling to start a fire to get the coal going. Dad had just bought a brand new axe, and it was a fairly large axe. I was using it to cut kindling. It was a little heavy for me because I was still in the first grade, therefore, only six years old.

Mama came by while I was trying to cut the kindling. She said, "Now Charles, if you're going to cut that kindling, you need to lay it down on the ground and stand back from it and hit it this way with the axe to split the boards." The kindling was made from boards Daddy had picked up somewhere.

That worked for a little bit, and then Earl came by. He said, "Charles, that's not the way to split that kindling." He held it up vertically and came down with the axe, picking the board up at the same time, hitting it on the ground to split it. He said, "Now that's the way to split that kindling."

Well, I should not have listened! I should have listened to my mother, and I didn't do what she asked me to. I tried it, and the axe being as heavy as it was, caused it to come right down on my left knuckles. I almost cut my index finger off with that axe. It split the joint in my finger and cut the other finger next to it a little bit. To this day, I have a scar where that happened. I couldn't hold the finger up, it was so near cut off, and the joint was split. Blood was squirting every time my heart would beat, because I had cut an artery.

It was about time for Daddy to come home from work, and all he had to do was walk across the street. Mama got him on that real soon. She said, "I think he needs to go to the doctor."

Daddy borrowed a car from one of the boarders because we didn't have a car. He took me to the old Rock Hill bank building where Dr. Bundy, the same doctor that saved my life, worked in an office on the top floor. We got there and walked in on the main floor, ready to get on the elevator. Dr. Bundy happened to be getting off the elevator as we were going to get on. Daddy said, "Dr. Bundy, we need your help."

He answered, "What have you got here?" He looked at my finger and said, "Oh, we need to fix that." We went up the elevator to his office, and he gave me two stitches to hold it together for healing. He did a smart thing. He was a good doctor in a lot of ways. He put a splint under my finger to hold it out straight so that joint would heal properly. I couldn't bend my finger after he did that, and I wasn't supposed to. My finger healed and I have never had a minute's trouble with it in any way, gripping anything or whatever, since that day. But it sure did scare me when I saw all that blood coming out of my finger. I just knew I had lost a finger.

My sweetheart at that time was Sara Lazenby. We were first grade sweethearts. The next day I didn't go to school because of that accident. Dean told Sara's sister what I had done, she told Sara, and Sara just cried and cried. See, I've had women crying over me many, many times.

I remember when Dr. Bundy was sewing me up. That fish-hook looking needle that he was using to stitch up my finger hurt, and he didn't have any way of deadening it. Dad said, "Charles, if you'll do this and not cry, I'll get you a cone of ice cream on the way home." I didn't cry; I wanted that ice cream so badly I didn't cry! Dr. Bundy said, "Well, he's not gonna' cry anyway. I sew all those Shaw boys up all the time, and they don't cry, so he's not gonna' cry either." That helped, because I took his word for it that I wouldn't cry. Dad kept his word, and we went by somewhere, and he bought me a big cone of ice cream.

We three boys were always trying to find something to do when we were out of school during the time we lived at 41 Community Street. We decided one day we were going to build a car. This would be a very crudely put together car, using scraps from the Aragon Mill scrap bin, croaker sacks on a wooden frame. Of course it would have no motor; we would push each other down the sidewalk in this car. Living as close as we did to the mill, we could go to the scrap metal bin where they threw machine parts. Like many other people, we would find stuff in that bin that we could use to build something. We were able to make the wheels out of gears, when we found four alike. They were okay—cast iron—until you happened to run over your bare foot, with the teeth on those gears cutting into your foot. That wasn't any fun at all!

The steering column was made out of a broom handle with a wagon wheel for the steering wheel. We had leather straps, belts I believe, wrapped around that broom handle in such a way that it was fastened to the front axle, and when you turned the steering wheel, the leather straps would wrap up on the wheel and pull the axle the way you wanted to go. However, we decided to make it more interesting. We wound the leather straps around that broom handle backward, which meant that when you turned to the right normally, it would go to the left instead. When we turned it to the left, the car would go to the right. We had a lot of fun with that. You can tell there were times we didn't have much else to do and needed something like that to pass the time of day!

Across the road, in front of the house, was a large field for the YMCA at the Aragon Mill village. There were some big oak trees in the edge of that field. I would scoot my wagon around, pretending I was collecting insurance, or whatever, and had a lot of fun with that. The field was very large, several acres, and it made a good playground for the boys and girls there on the mill village. We had some of the best football and baseball games there you've ever seen.

The large building that was across the street from our house, in the edge of that field, was called the YMCA building. It may have at one time been a Young Men's Christian Association, but the mill company built it mainly to provide recreation for the people who lived on the mill village. This was more than for children and young people. There was recreation for adults at the same time—dominoes, card games, etc. for the adults. They would meet there just before time to go into the mill and work, and it was just across the street from the mill.

We also built a boat, made from scrap lumber when they were re-doing part of the mill. We were able to get some of that lumber, knock the nails out of it and build a boat. We got tar and melted it and poured it on the bottom of the boat to make it waterproof. We called it Seemore Boat—you could "see more" tar than you could boat—but at least it didn't leak! We took the boat to Taylors Creek, which was a fair-sized stream, not too far out of town, and we played with that boat in the stream. When we finished playing with it each time, we would put some large rocks in it and weight it down to the bottom so it wouldn't get stolen.

The mill company also provided a golf course, which was the same stretch of land just across the creek from the mill where they were able to make a baseball field with a fence around it to keep the cows out. They had a lot of good baseball games as part of the recreation between the different mill companies in Rock Hill. There were about 15 or 20 mills in that town, doing textiles.

In that same cow pasture, in addition to the baseball field, they had a nine-hole golf course. You sometimes had to scare the cows out of the way to keep from hitting them with a golf ball. That's not all you had to be careful about—you also had to watch where you walked in the cow pasture!

We didn't give birthday presents very often when I was growing up, but I remember one that I got on my seventh birthday. Dad decided to give me a toy golf club, and it had a little rubber ball with it. There was a lot of golfing going on in that cow pasture. Daddy took up golfing. Some of the golfers lived with us. I remember the name Carl Jordan, a man who was a professional golfer for a while, but he had come to Rock Hill and was boarding with us. He didn't play in that cow pasture very much; he usually went to the country club. He won all kinds of trophies at the club.

I recall one of the times that Dad took me with him when he went to the golf course there in the pasture. I took my toy golf club and ball, and I would hit mine along the way as he was working his ball through the course. The fairway had all kinds of weeds; it wasn't a nice smooth area like your professional golf courses are today. I lost my ball, and I couldn't find it. Dad took time from playing golf that day, and we looked and looked, and finally found it. I was just about in tears because I thought it was so great that I had a present like that, my own golf club and ball.

The mill village could be a rough place to live. I remember a time that we were watching a ballgame between two of the mill companies there in that ball field. There were two men that had a falling out about something—it had nothing to do with the ballgame. It was something that happened at home, or at least not there at the ball field. Those two men were slugging it out. They were fighting just like you see on television, on westerns and so forth.

Another interesting thing about that was, a week or so after that fight, one of those men was found dead out in the edge of Rock Hill in the woods. Everybody immediately assumed that the other guy who was in the fight with him had killed him, but that turned out not to be so. We also had a couple that lived on the village that had a falling out between man and wife. The man shot his wife with a shotgun, right in the chest. He served time for that, of course. On the same street we lived on, another man was spending time in the penitentiary for somewhat the same kind of crime.

During those same 41 Community Street years, we bought groceries for the family at Dabney's Grocery Store, down about three or four blocks from the house. There was one time Mama made a list of several items she needed for supper that night. She asked me to go to Dabney's and get those items. Mr. Dabney had trouble reading Mama's writing.

She could write real fast, but it was kind of strung out in such a way that was hard to read, even after I learned to read really well. He was trying to make out a couple of the items she wanted. He asked me if I knew what it was, and I said, "No, I don't know." I had just heard that Mama and Daddy had celebrated their 18th wedding anniversary. I said, "Mr. Dabney, you're gonna' have to do the best you can with that. Mama and Daddy have been married 18 years." He laughed and laughed and laughed and later told Dad and Mama about that the next time they were in the store. I don't know why that had anything to do with Mama's handwriting, but he laughed about it anyway.

The house we lived in there on Community Street had a porch that went halfway around the house. It went across the front of the house, back a little ways, to the door to go into the house, then to the right and all the length of the house on the right side. This made a good place for us to play during bad weather.

Daddy decided to be really practical one time at Christmas, not that he wasn't ordinarily, but he decided to buy a set of woodworking tools for us to have a shop. The shop was on the end of that large porch. It wasn't enclosed like a room; it was open just as a porch would be. Interestingly enough, we weren't concerned about the tools getting stolen.

Earl and Dean had been making whatnot's out of quarter-inch plywood as a part of Vacation Bible School hand work. This was one of the reasons Dad decided to give us the tools. He would go to Rock Hill Lumber Company, where they made cabinets, and he would buy a bunch of quarter-inch plywood for almost nothing. They were glad to get rid of it. He would bring all that plywood to that porch, and we made whatnot's and tried to sell them to make a little money.

We made a number of whatnot's that we did sell. In fact, my second grade school teacher came to visit, as the teachers did in those days, just to get acquainted with the parents and be able to talk to them about any problem the child was having in school. Miss Brasington was my second grade teacher, and while she was there, I tried to sell her a whatnot. Mama shamed me, and I gave it to her instead. You know, that did not get me a higher grade in school. She was too honest for that.

Dad used that little shop on the end of the porch to do some things for the house. One of the things he built, that we still have in our basement here in Chunns Cove, was a chifferobe. It had four drawers in it and a place to hang clothes on the right side. There were drawers on the left, clothes on the right. It's still very useful for me in my shop. I ended up with it to use for storing tools and other items in my woodworking shop. I never open that chiffarobe that I don't think about Daddy. He made that piece with hand tools. We did not have any machines like I have in my woodworking shop now. That made it very interesting.

We also had a bookcase that was called a desk (it would open up like a desk) that he made out of scrap boxes before we moved to Rock Hill. That item was used the whole time Mom and Dad kept house. I believe my nephew Tim, Earl's boy, has that now.

A scary thing happened while we lived there on Community Street. It was a Sunday evening, and we three boys were at home. Dad was at church. I don't remember where Mama was, but she went to Cowpens fairly often to check on her mother, who was in poor health and had some age on her too. We boys were probably listening to Sunday night radio programs, maybe *Jack Benny* or *Amos and Andy*. I don't remember. We heard a knock at the door, and all three of us went to see who was there. When we opened the door, there stood a young man our family knew pretty well. We knew him and his brothers and his parents.

Earl, being the oldest, did not invite him in because he could tell that he was drinking. In fact, he was drunk enough that he didn't know where he was. He told us that he wanted to see our daddy. We told him that Dad was not there, that he was at church. The man said he was going to "whup" him. When Earl asked him why he wanted to whup our daddy, he told us that Daddy had called the police to arrest a buddy of his. Earl asked, "Why did Daddy call the police on him?" The man said, "I don't know why, but I'm gonna' whup your daddy anyway!"

We couldn't call Daddy; we didn't have phones in those days, and there was no way we could get in touch with him. The only time we ever had even a land-type phone on the mill village was there at Community Street. The only reason we had that was because we had those boarders, and they wanted to pay for it.

The reason Daddy called the police the night the man was speaking of, was that his friend was driving a car and he was drinking. We had a wide place in front of our house over to the YMCA building that I've spoken about. He was buzzing around and around in the car. It was a dirt street, and he was kicking up a lot of dust. He'd run up on the curb, just acting really unruly. Daddy went in the house and called the police. They came out and arrested the guy and took him in. So this fellow was going to "whup" Daddy for calling the police.

It was past time for Dad to come home from church, and we were all wishing he would come on. However, we were afraid if he came while the fellow was there, he might be in a whole lot of trouble. Those people in those days would pull out a knife and work you over real good. We were scared to death that this might happen to Daddy.

Before the man left the house, he was walking off the porch, and we looked down the street and saw a car coming. It happened to be Preacher Boone, our pastor, and Daddy, and of all people, the third person was the fellow's brother. I will always believe God put the brother in that car that night.

When the man saw who it was after the car stopped, he realized Daddy was in the car. He said, "Crocker, get out here. I'm gonna whup you for calling the police on my buddy." The man's brother was in the back seat of Preacher Boone's car. He immediately got out and walked over to his brother, took him by the arm, and said, "You ain't gon' whup nobody." He took him by the arm, led him across the street, and down through the Y field, walking him home. He lived on the mill village himself.

We were glad to get Daddy in the house. We'd been scared to death while this was taking place. I'll never forget how Earl held that screen door latch to where it wouldn't open. He was taking care of his two younger brothers; however Earl was only about 12 years old at that time, and I was about six years old. (I have purposely not named the man who came to our door nor his brother because as he got older and matured, he was not that mean or hateful kind of person; he was always highly respected.)

We lived at 41 Community Street for about three years. As I explained earlier, the house was for Bessie Allen, but since she was a single person, they had us moved to that house, and we were keeping boarders. Bessie Allen became ill. Her heart condition got worse, and she moved back to Greenville. That opened the way for us to move somewhere else on the mill village if we wanted to do so.

Earl, Charles and Dean on the front steps
of their home at 41 Community Street

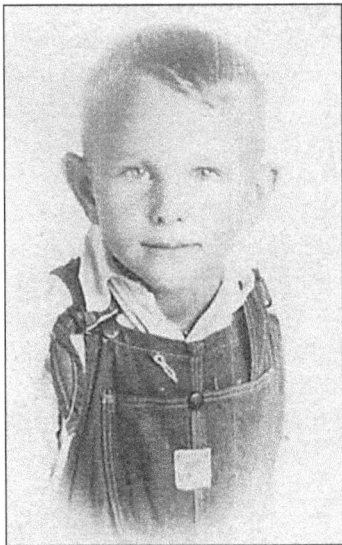

First grade

Second grade

4

Northside Baptist Church

Northside Baptist Church was organized in 1908 to serve as a place of worship for the Aragon Mill village and the Industrial Mill village. It was located exactly between those two villages. There was also the Bethel Methodist Church, which was just a stone's throw away from Northside Baptist, and it also served as a place of worship for the Aragon and Industrial villages.

When we moved to the Aragon Mill village, we began attending and worshiping at Northside. Most people did not pronounce the "th" in Northside; they would say "Nor'side". I never did ask why we changed churches just because Daddy had changed work, however, it made sense to go to a church that was only a block or two away. It was an excellent church. At that time, Dad had already sold his car which he had to have selling insurance, and we had to walk to church. Walking two or three blocks was very different from walking all the way to downtown, which would have been a mile or two.

Northside Baptist was originally in the same block as the mill. It was a wooden frame building with a bell up in a tower. That bell was so heavy that it took several boys to ring the bell at the time it was supposed to be rung. They would get it going and ride the rope up and down. The bell was large enough to carry the boys up and down.

The church members were thinking about building a new church building because the old wood framed building needed a lot of work. The pastor felt that if we had a better worship place and Sunday School place, we would reach more people, which proved to be true.

The baptistry in the old building was right in the middle of the rostrum area, right behind where the pulpit would be for preaching. The heater to heat the water was down in a kind of basement area under the church. That heating element caused a fire at one time, and the church caught fire. Someone found it in time to put the fire out before it did much damage. The fire department had not arrived because the blaze had not gotten that far along, and the people in the area were able to put the fire out. Preacher Boone was an old Irishman who said what he thought. He asked the guys what in the world they put it out for, "Don't you know we're trying to build a new building?" Of course he was going on with his Irish foolishness.

The new site the members were contemplating for the new building was on the other side of the railroad. This is probably what Dad was busy with at the church the evening the angry young man came looking for him, and why he was later coming home. Dad was always very much a part of anything big like that the church was doing. They were probably talking about ways to make it all happen. This was about 1939.

Dad was so much a part of it that when they started construction, he promised he would do the electrical wiring for the whole building, which he did. Dad had worked at Huntington & Guerry Electrical Company in Spartanburg, and had learned all he needed to know about doing such a thing. He promised to wire the church if the church would buy all the fixtures, of course. The church had 300 outlets (any place in the building which used electricity was called an outlet). There were 300 of them in the church. Daddy would work eight hours in the mill on the first shift, from 8:00 until

4:00, then he would go down, cross the railroad, work until about suppertime, go home to eat supper, then go back to the church and work at night. Many times he worked until 11 and 12 o'clock, trying to get all that wiring done.

Dean and I helped Daddy a good bit. I was not able to do as much as Dean because I was younger. Mainly what Dean and I did was bore holes through wooden braces and so forth to run wires through, like Daddy wanted them.

The funniest thing happened one day. Daddy had Dean boring holes through the ceiling joists in the sanctuary so he could run wires for lights that were going to be between the windows—sconces, they were. Dad happened to walk out in the sanctuary to see how Dean was coming with his assignment. He looked up and saw Dean walking around up in the ceiling joists to bore those holes. That sanctuary was a good 20 feet up to the ceiling. Dean had a two by four stuck through his overall straps, across his back. Dad looked up at him, and said, "Dean, why in the world have you got that two-by-four in your overalls like that?" Dean said, "Huh! If I fall, that two-by-four's going to catch me, keeping me from falling down through these ceiling joists!" Daddy said, "You're a smart young man!" He was.

An interesting thing happened to me while that church was being built. The church was fairly close to a patch of woods. I had been down in the woods with my single shot BB gun, shooting birds. I came back by the church, and I was afraid Daddy would scold me if I went in that building with a rifle. The building wasn't finished, but it was going to be a place of worship. I was afraid he wouldn't want me to do that, so I went into the basement area, and hid my rifle behind the boiler. The church was going to be heated by coal heat, with a boiler furnishing steam to radiators in the church. I went back to it later, after I had gone to check on Daddy to see if I could help him. My rifle wasn't there.

There was only one other person that knew I put that rifle there, and he lived fairly close, just a few houses from the church. He was a boy about my age or a little older, and I asked him if he got my rifle. He said no he didn't. I said "You had to have gotten it because nobody else knew it was there

but you." He never did own up to that, and I never did get my
rifle back. Years later, I was down in that area of the church,
after I was grown man. I walked back in there where the
boiler was, to see if somehow that rifle had slid down under
the equipment, but it hadn't. So I never did get my rifle back.

The old Northside Baptist Church and the new building
were close to the railroad. Just across the street, in both cases,
was Southern Railroad. There was a long freight train that
came through every Sunday, about the time Preacher Boone
was doing the sermon. By law, the engineer had to blow
the whistle for the crossing that was right there close to the
church. It seemed like the whistle lasted a whole lot longer
than it really did, because Preacher Boone would just have to
stop preaching while it was happening. One time I remember
him saying, "That's the first train I've ever known that had
a whistle as long as the track!"

Daddy decided he could do something about that. He
had a way of thinking, "there's always a way" just like I have
always had. He happened to be in the downtown area one
day when that train came through on a weekday, not Sunday.
The train stopped to shift cars, etc., and Dad walked over to
the engine and climbed up to talk to the engineer. He said,
"You know, down the track here a ways, right in the edge of
town, we have a little church, Northside Baptist Church. We
are trying to do the best we can to have good services and
good worship. When our pastor is preaching, we're trying
to hear him. When you come by about that time on Sunday
mornings, it's hard to hear him when you're blowing the
whistle. He has to stop preaching until you finish and the train
gets by. It would be good if there's any way you could see fit
to keep the law with the way you have to blow the whistle,
but not hold it so long." The engineer said, "I think I can do
that. I'll do what I can." Daddy explained exactly where the
church was, and the engineer said he'd be looking for it.

The next Sunday, we heard the train coming. Daddy, of
course, was listening more to that than he was the sermon
probably. When it got to where the engineer had to blow the
whistle, it was just a little "toot-toot". He just barely blew it
enough to get by. Daddy said, "Well, it worked."

Northside Baptist Church was good for our family. Dean and I accepted Christ at Northside in the old church. We were having a revival, preached by Walter Boone, who happened to be the son of J.J. Boone, our pastor. It was a long, two-week revival. A lot of people accepted Christ and moved their membership into our church too. One of the things that made this interesting was that when the invitation was given the night Dean and I accepted Christ, neither of us knew that the other was going. We went from different places in the church down to the front to meet the pastor and to say that we wanted to accept Christ and join the church. We did a lot of things together, which I'll talk about a little later.

We accepted Christ just after I was nine years old. (Earl had already accepted Christ and joined the church at an earlier date. He was very much a part of that church while he was growing up.) It was a summer revival. The new church building was in the process of being built at that time. Promotion Day happened every year at the first of September, meaning the day children would be promoted from one department to another. I was supposed to be promoted, but we decided that everyone would wait until we were in the new building. That way, everyone would move into their new areas. Sometime in the fall of that year, we went through a time of promotion and ended up in our new departments.

Dean and I were baptized in the old church. It was the type of baptistry that the floor of the rostrum opened up, and there were steps going down, and the water was right there. If you were sitting up in the edge of the choir, on each side of the baptistry, you could see people go down in the water and come back up. We *knew* they were baptized.

There were a lot of good people at Northside who cared about children, hoping they would live the life they should live and accept Christ, and be an influence to others. One person I think of first is Perry Faile. Not a day passes that I don't quote him in some way. He loved children. He was the Junior Department Superintendent when I was coming through the Sunday School.

Perry spent a lot of time with children. When a lot of other children were getting in trouble, doing things they shouldn't be doing, he would just about always have a group, boys especially, going hiking or fishing. We would go down below the dam on the Catawba River. This was a dam that furnished power to part of Charlotte and all of Rock Hill. We would fish below the dam and catch bream.

He was a master fisherman when it came to fishing for bream. He could put his hook in the water and just pull out one after the other. I would ease my hook over fairly close to where his was without getting in his fishing hole, and just sit there and watch that cork, and never get a bite! I would say, "Perry, how are you catching those fish like that?" "Well Charlie, you gotta' hold your mouth right."

He would pull up really small fish, and he'd put them on his line and put it back in the water. I would say, "Perry, you're not going to string that little ol' bream up are you? Isn't that too small?" He'd say, "Huh. He bit my hook didn't he? If he's big enough to bite my hook, he's big enough to eat!" I would say, "I don't know how you do it, but you're a good fisherman."

Perry told me a story about Jesus and the disciples who were fishing. He'd say, "Charlie, you know there was a fishing trip one day, and they weren't catching any fish at all. And the Lord appeared and told them what they were doing wrong. He said, 'You're fishing on the wrong side of the boat.' They put their nets on the other side and pulled in more fish than they could get in the boat almost. Jesus said, 'Follow me, and I'll make you to become fishers of men.'" And at that point, Perry would say something like, "And Charlie, he'll make a fisherman out of you, fishing for men, if you'll follow him and give your life to him." I have tried to do that through music for many, many years. Perry Faile influenced my life more than any other person, second only to my dad.

My becoming a Christian in this church and being influenced by so many good people helped to guide me in following the Lord's will throughout my life, as I'll share in the next chapters.

Northside Baptist Church, about 1941,
with Mr. Mullis' Ford parked in front

Northside Baptist Church Vacation Bible School.
Dean is holding the Christian flag.
Charles is two faces to the left of Dean and slightly above.

5

84 Frayser Street

After living on Community Street, we moved to 84 Frayser Street. The Garrisons lived there, and shortly after Bessie Allen left us, they built a house away from the mill village. This cleared the way for us to move into their former house. The mill company kept their promise. This was a very ideal place to live.

We moved to a house, but in our minds, as boys, we were moving to heaven because all the things that cramped us and made life difficult for us at 41 Community Street were wiped out completely at 84 Frayser Street. The house was at the end of a street. When you went any further around the side of the house and out to the right, on a dirt road, it was the middle of a 17-acre field. There was a patch of woods beyond that, probably another 10 or 12 acres—an ideal place for boys to have a good time. We squirrel hunted in those woods and rabbit hunted in the field. I caught rabbits in a rabbit box there. We just had a good time. When I think back to when I was a boy, the place that I think of most when I say "going home in my mind" I'm thinking about 84 Frayser Street.

That also seemed to be the time when our family came together without so much hardship. We enjoyed being together more there because of where the house was and so forth. The only thing I can think of that changed that feeling was the fact that not long after we moved there, Earl joined the Navy. Pearl Harbor had already happened. He finished high school in June of '41 and joined the Navy in November of '42. This was extremely hard on Mama, because she was thinking back on the fact that she lost three brothers during World War I. All she could think was, "I might lose a son."

One of the things we enjoyed doing in that 17-acre field was flying kites. The field was big enough that the least little wind would fly a kite. We made kites out of straw and newspaper. We would get a bobbin of thread out of the mill, which would fly a kite sometimes a thousand feet out from us. When we finished with that, we'd just turn it loose and not even try to wind it in. Some of the kites we bought, but most of them we just made ourselves. When we were told to "go fly a kite," we knew how to do it.

The field was owned by a lawyer there in Rock Hill. He raised horses and cattle, but not in that field. However, he did grow some grass, which made hay for the cow feed, and there where haystacks all over the place. A pole would be put up, and straw and cow silage would be put up around that post; it would go up about eight or ten feet. This made a good thing on which to play. We played King of the Hill and whatever we wanted to enjoy each other on those haystacks.

We did all sorts of things in that field and in the woods. We would hunt squirrels in the woods, hunt rabbits in the field, and shoot dove. It made a good place for us to shoot a .22 rifle without endangering anybody's life except our own, but we were really careful. We had learned gun safety and later received a Marksman merit badge in Scouts. We were taught more about gun safety than we were about how to shoot a target. I built rabbit boxes, really a rabbit trap. It was a square box about three feet long, and made in such a way that when the rabbit went in to get the meat, he would bump a trigger which made a door fall behind him, and he couldn't get out. I caught a rabbit the first night that I set a trap, and we had that sucker for Sunday dinner!

One of the things we did with the BB gun that we should not have done (because it was a little bit dangerous) was shoot snuff cans off each other's head (not a .22). We also had our back turned, and if we missed the can, it wouldn't hurt us too bad. But we didn't miss it.

There was one thing we did in shooting that we'll never do again. We would take .22 cartridges and stick them in a clay bank of dirt and shoot the back of them with the BB gun, making the cartridge explode, just as if it were in the .22 rifle. It would ignite the powder in the cartridge. The only problem with that was, the hull that contained the powder was lighter than the bullet, and the hull would come back toward you more than the bullet would go in the ground.

Dean and I were doing that one day. We had shot several times, and the .22 hull would come back and hit our britches leg or go sailing off into the air. Dean did it one more time, and this time, the empty hull came back and caught him just above the right eye. If it had been an inch lower, it would have put his eye out. The empty hull was sharp enough that it cut a pretty good sized gash in Dean's head. Dean grabbed his hand and put it over his eye and the place where the hull had hit him. He said, "Charles, Charles, did he get me, did he get me, did he get me?" I said, "I don't know Dean. I can't see for your hand." Mr. H. L. Shaw heard that story and nearly every time I was around him after that until I was a grown man, he would once in a while say, "Charles, did he get me, did he get me, did he get me?" Then he'd answer and say, "I don't know Dean. I can't see for your hand."

We were afraid to go home for fear we would be scolded really badly or even get a whipping. We went down the street. Dean was bleeding profusely, but we soaked up the blood with a tissue or handkerchief. We started playing marbles. You might know, here came Daddy, after we'd been up the street a while. He was coming home from the mill. He looked over and saw Dean's head. He said, "Dean, what in the world is wrong with your head?" Dean said, "Well, we may as well go ahead and tell you." He told Daddy what happened. Of course, he insisted on Dean going right on home to treat and doctor that gash in his head. We learned a lesson and never did that again. We would tell boys who enjoyed doing that sort of thing not to ever do it, and we would tell them what happened to Dean. We should have known that hull was a lot lighter than the bullet, and it would tend to come back toward the rifle more than the bullet would go in the ground.

You remember that World War II had already begun when the Japanese bombed Pearl Harbor on December 7, 1941. That meant the entire world was at war. We boys felt it necessary to guard that field because we just knew that the Japanese or the Germans were going to be coming into that field just any day. So in order to do this, we organized a small group of boys called Marine Juniors, and we guarded that field. We lived at the end of the street, and that field was next to our house.

We had two chinaberry trees in the back yard, and the one that was closest to the field had grown in such a way that it was easy to build a platform up in the tree, which we did. We had all kinds of things up there to pretend we were guarding that field. We had a telescope, a spotlight, and several other things. Of course, the Japanese and the Germans were thousands of miles away, but in our mind, they were going to be coming in that field just any day, and we had to be ready for them.

We had training sessions for the boys in the group, teaching them how to shoot. We spent time studying aircraft, and we got all sorts of pictures of different kinds of war planes, and we were going to be able to identify any plane that flew over that field. We'd know what it was, whether a B-26 bomber, B-25 bomber, flying fortress, which was a B-24, a B-29, or others. We could see them flying over, sometimes flying out of Charlotte, when there was a military air base up there. It may not have been important to anybody else, but we had to know those planes so we could know if it was a Japanese plane or a German plane.

Now it's time for me to tell a story about a B-26 bomber that came over. We looked up, we identified it, and we pretended it was an enemy plane (of course it wasn't), and we pretended like we were shooting it down. Would you believe—true story—that plane started falling while we were watching it. It was falling end over end, not sailing down like it was going to land, but it just started falling. That plane had run out of fuel. The pilot, we learned later, was trying to make it back to Charlotte where they had the right kind of fuel to put in the plane, and he crashed in the edge of Ebenezer, a little community that you went into immediately after driving up the York Highway out of Rock Hill. Ebenezer was the little community where my wife Mae lived when we started going together.

We saw the plane fall, and a few seconds after that, there was black smoke coming up where the plane went down. We had a feeling that plane had crashed, and it had. We decided to go over there, but by the time we got ready to drive over there and check on it, there were sirens going, like ambulance, police, etc. Word had already gotten to proper authorities that the plane had crashed, and all this was happening. There were fire trucks there with firemen to try to put the fire out. There was an incendiary bomb on that plane, and it was burning, an extremely hot fire.

When we got to where we could see, the plane had crashed in a little thicket of pine trees, and I saw the most pitiful sight I've ever seen. I still remember exactly what it was. The pilot had tried to bail out, and the way the plane was falling, there was no way he could get a door open and get out in time. He was not all that high in altitude to start with, so I believe he was coming down to try to land that plane somewhere in that area. The pilot's parachute had burned and the cinders were out behind the pilot, and you could tell it didn't have time to open. He looked like he had just been cooked and baked. When they rolled him over to wrap him in a piece of canvas, his arms and elbows came up just like a roasted chicken's legs come right off. It was an awful sight. After quite a while, they got the fire out and did the necessary things to take the body where it needed to go.

Another B-26 bomber landed in Rock Hill. The pilot was having mechanical problems with the plane, so he brought the plane down on York Avenue, which was a long, wide street, really flat, over around the fairgrounds in Rock Hill. This was later called Cherry Road. There was a big write-up in the paper about the fact that this pilot had taken the plane down and landed safely on York Avenue.

While working on this autobiography, I happened to be talking about this story with Mae's brother, Fant. We were discussing how the plane needed some kind of part in order to get back in the air. Fant explained to me that the mechanic who helped find the part they needed was Mae's Uncle Jim Steele. I thought that was kind of interesting and did not know about his involvement until recently.

They brought fuel from Charlotte to refuel the plane, and people were saying, "How is he going to get this thing out of here?" Well, the street was lined with people on both sides to watch that plane take off. He revved that engine up, threw the pitch to the props, and he took that two-engine bomber up from York Avenue. He didn't hit any telephone wires or posts, and he went on back to Charlotte and landed. For a town like Rock Hill, in those days, that was exciting stuff happening.

We also made a large slingshot, taken from the fork of a fair-sized tree, and great big strips of rubber, fastened to a board in such a way we could shoot large rocks. That was our cannon gun in that field. It was just like a slingshot you could have in your hand, but it was a great big thing. We figured it would scare the Japanese or the Germans half to death when they saw it, I guess.

I saved my money for a while and bought a Red Ryder Carbine, a BB gun. We called it an air rifle, but BB gun is the more common term, I think. This was about the time it was getting fairly close to Christmas. Earl had joined the Navy at age 17, and he had timed his joining to be able to come home after his boot training. He went to Norfolk, Virginia, to a naval base there, and that's where he did boot camp. This is the training all the sailors would take, getting them ready for further training, in which they would specialize.

The fact that it was getting close to Christmas, I was asked by members of the family—Uncle Deck and Aunt Annie Mae (Mama's brother and his wife), Uncle Roy and Aunt Venice (Daddy's sister and her husband) what I wanted for Christmas. I said, "I don't want anything but air rifle shot. Just give me plenty of air rifle shot so I can kill these old sparrows that are around the house."

It came time for our family gathering, which included the five of us with Uncle Deck and Aunt Annie Mae and

Uncle Roy and Aunt Venice, neither of whom had children. They always gave us toys or whatever for Christmas. By this time we were not getting toys, but a little more serious stuff. Earl was sick with the flu when he got home, and he almost used up his boot leave getting over the flu, but he made it. When we were distributing the presents at that gathering, I was handed a small package from Earl. I could tell by the shape of it, that it most likely was a box of air rifle shot. Those boxes were shaped about like a shotgun shell, except it would have BB pellets in it. I thought to myself, "Now Earl could do better than that!" I realized all I wanted was air rifle shot, but I thought I might get a *little* something else that I didn't ask for. When I unwrapped it, it was a box of air rifle shot, but it had a $2 dollar bill wrapped around the outside of it. At that time, I had never seen a two dollar bill, but I learned that servicemen, in many cases, were paid with cash money, which quite often would include two dollar bills. That doesn't sound like much so far as a gift is concerned now, but in that day, that was a very nice gift. I could pour a whole box of those shot in my BB gun and not have to reload it. I could just cock it and shoot, cock it and shoot.

We had a dog that I haven't mentioned, named Tip. His name was Tippie when he was a small pup, but when he got older, we called him Tip. He was really Dean's dog, given to him by Roy and Venice, because Tip's mother was Roy and Venice's dog, Trixie. When Tip saw me come out of the house with my Red Ryder Carbine, he would jump up and down all around me. He knew what I was about to do, and he wanted to go with me.

Just to play with him, and I guess it was kind of cruel, I'd say, "No Tip, you can't go." His ears would droop, and he'd sit back on his haunches, and he'd watch me walk away. I would turn around, and his ears would go up like "I'm about to be called!" I'd say, "No Tip, you can't come." I would walk on for a ways. The dirt road went up in the edge of that field, toward a couple of trees, and if I'd gone much farther, I would have been out of sight. But every time I would turn around, his ears would cock up like he expected to be called. I did that two or three times, and then finally I'd say, "Well, I guess it's okay. Come on!" That's all it took. He would come running, just happy as a lark. That's just a story of a boy and his dog.

I also had a cat, a full-blooded Persian cat that Bessie Allen had given me for Christmas when we lived down on Community Street. After several years, Tabby died. When she died, the lady who worked at Dickert's store on the block behind our house, heard about it. She said to me, "I've got several cats, and I'd be glad to give you one. One of them is a black cat with four white feet, really beautiful." I asked Mama about it. I said "Mrs. Robinson wants to give me a cat." Mama said, "It's all right if it's not a female cat." Tabby had had kittens, and we couldn't get rid of them fast enough.

I told Mrs. Robinson what Mama said. She said, "Oh, it's a tom cat." A few months later, that tomcat had a litter of kittens! I went out to Dickert's store, and I said it where a good number of workers heard me, "Mrs. Robinson! Do you know that tom cat you gave me?" She said, "Yeah, how's he doing?" And I said, "Well he just had a litter of about a half dozen kittens!" The meat cutter, Mr. Emmett Hyatt, nearly rolled in the floor he laughed so hard. Mrs. Robinson apologized, but she was more embarrassed than anything.

About this time, Grandma and Papa Ledford lived at Carpenter's Knob. One of the things I remember doing when we three boys would go to Grandma's house was shooting our slingshots at lizards. One day we were walking along a nearby wagon road and I thought I had seen a lizard about 25 or 30 feet away. I kept watching for it to see if I could find it again without leaving the road. Earl and Dean kept on walking and left me, and they were on down the road at least 100 to 200 yards when I finally saw the lizard. I shot him with my slingshot, and I got him!

I went on down the road, calling for Earl and Dean. They stopped and waited on me, and when I got there, I said, "I got him! I got him!"

They said, "You got what?"

"That lizard I was watching for! I watched him go up the tree a little ways, and I shot him, and he fell off in the leaves!"

They said, "Aw, you can't hit a lizard like that!"

I said "Yes, I did too!" We had a real argument; I was about ready to shoot *them* with my slingshot! Earl and Dean were not really calling me a liar. They were just teasing me the way they did many, many times.

I remember when I was afraid of cows. I was not around cows very much when we were at home. They were in a pasture furnished by the mill company, but we did not have a cow, therefore, when I got around them at Grandma's, I was afraid of them. I wasn't more than about six or seven years old at the most, so a cow was an awfully large animal to me.

We were down playing in the creek, the same creek we went down to when I shot the lizard, and my attention was drawn to the stuff we were doing in the creek, trying to build a dam to dam up the water and make a swimming hole. There was a molasses mill there we played with some too, so I was not paying attention much to things happening around me. I happened to look behind me, and there was a cow standing there, not too far from where I was, moving toward me. It frightened me quite a bit. I ran to a nearby pine tree, and I went up that pine tree like a squirrel! Earl and Dean both said they never in this world thought I would be able to climb a tree like that! You know a pine tree doesn't have many low limbs, so it was a matter of just wrapping my arms around the tree, and using my feet to scoot up that tree. I got high enough that I didn't worry about the cow anyway!

Following the episode with the lizard, we went on down the creek, and came up on a large pile of sawdust. It must have been 10 or 15 feet high and was made by a saw mill that Papa allowed to come in there to saw some timber. In a saw mill like that, there's a chain that will carry sawdust from where the actual cutting is taking place over to a place to dump it. This had made a really high sawdust pile. It was a good place for three boys to have fun. We didn't know it was there, or we would have been there sooner.

We started playing on that sawdust, playing King of the Hill or whatever came to our minds, trying to see who could stay on the top. Of course, I didn't have much hope of winning the game; I was such a little fellow. However, playing in the sawdust like that, it got all in our clothes. The only way we had of getting the sawdust out, and to play without getting more in our clothes, was to take our clothes off! You need to know that this was way back in the woods, and we didn't worry too much about anybody coming by or being arrested for indecent exposure. After we stripped all of our clothes off, we *really* had fun in that sawdust pile!

We saw something very strange in part of the sawdust. It looked like something growing out of it. There was a bunch of sprouts of some kind that were growing out of that sawdust, and we were fascinated by them. We reached down to pull out two or three of those sprouts, and they pulled up a piece of a sweet potato. So again, we'd found us something to play with. We pulled those sweet potatoes up and started throwing them at each other. It's a wonder we didn't get hurt at that, but we didn't. We threw potatoes, and we threw sawdust, and we just about leveled that sawdust pile with all our foolishness.

When we finished playing there, we left and went on our way, on down kind of in the direction of Grandma and Papa's. A day or so later, Papa questioned us, asking if we were over in the area of the saw mill. We said we were. He said, "Did you see my sweet potatoes?" We said, "Uh oh. He's got us!"

We were ignorant little farmers, but he was a very skilled farmer, and he knew about things like that. We thought it was just pieces of sweet potatoes that somebody just left there accidentally. We came to find out that this was his sweet potato bed, and we learned that you have to set out sprouts; you don't set out sweet potatoes like you do Irish potatoes. You have to put the potatoes in something like that sawdust to cause them to sprout, and that's what we saw sticking out of the sawdust pile.

Of course, we apologized to Papa and told him we didn't know what we were doing. We were just having fun. We didn't know that was how you grew sweet potatoes. He was the kind of guy who just laughed about it; he didn't seem to get mad at us. It's a wonder he didn't.

Well, I think it's time for a ghost story. A ghost story, but it's also a true story. All my stories are true—if you don't believe me, just ask me! My choir always enjoyed my true Rock Hill stories. Anytime I had a few minutes before entering a service with the choir, I would offer to tell a "Rock Hill" story. When I did, they started getting up and acting like they were going out!

Back to the story. I was always tinkering with something I was making or just enjoying the things a boy usually enjoys. I found a table knife—I don't recall now where it was in relation to the house, and that doesn't matter. I just know it was not one from in our house or Mama would have had a fit. I found the table knife and decided I was going to make me a hunting knife out of it. After all, I had a Red Ryder Carbine, and I needed a hunting knife to go on my belt to go along with it.

I was tinkering with that knife, trying to put a sharp edge on it. I wrapped the handle with tape, and I was going to make me a sheath for it. Mom and Dad were about to leave the house and go down about a block and a half to Roy and Venice's for a little visit. They left me at home because I wanted to work on my knife. I was in the kitchen where we did everything else, and I was trying to sharpen the knife and make a point on it.

All of a sudden, something hit the screen wire over the kitchen window. This was in the summertime, and the windows were open, but we had screens, of course, on the outside. I looked over that way, and I didn't see anything, but it frightened me just a little bit because it sounded like somebody had walked up there and hit the screen wire.

Well, I went back to working on my knife, and it happened again. I was a little more frightened this time, being at home by myself, and I had no telephone to where I could call Mama and Daddy and tell them about it. I was about eleven or twelve years old at that time, I think, still young enough that I could be frightened over something like that. Quite honestly, I was a little afraid to go out of the house on that side and try to see if anyone was there at the window.

I went out through the front door, down the steps to the sidewalk, and down that sidewalk I ran, just as hard as I could go! I wasn't about to let anybody get me! If they were going to abduct me or shoot me, or whatever, they were going to have to catch me first! That would have been hard to do in those days. I probably was barefooted, and I could run like a striped haint [ghost]!

I went down the street and around the corner, just a short distance to Venice's house. I told Mom and Dad about what had happened, and of course, they made little of it, "Aw, there's nothing to that!" I said, "Well, I don't know what made that noise, but it sounded like somebody walked up and hit the screen wire with their hand. And I don't know why anybody would do that just to scare me, because no one knew I was the only one there." It didn't seem right that they would go to the trouble to frighten me. Mama and Daddy said, "We're going to be here another little bit, then go home. Why don't you go on back up that way and finish working on your knife." I said, "I'll try that."

I went down a half a block, down to the corner (they usually had street lights at the corners and a few along the streets on the mill village). There happened to be two or three of my buddies, Dopey Jordan, that I've mentioned, was there, the Price boy and a couple of other guys, just standing there like boys will do, talking about most anything that would come up. I interrupted them long enough to tell them what was going on. I said, "I don't know what it was that hit that screen, but it scared me." Dopey Jordan wasn't afraid of anything, although he was a small boy and never did grow up to be very big. He said, "Let's go up there and see if we can figure it out." I said, "I'll go if y'all will go with me." They said, "Yeah, we'll go." We went up the street, and I made it clear that we lived at the end of the street, which made anything like this happening even more frightening. We had a street light almost in front of our house, but the street lights on a mill village were not all that bright.

We stopped one house down from my house. I looked and I could see a head moving and somebody sitting on our front porch. Mama always had a lot of good sized flowers on the porch, and this head I saw moving was kind of between two of the flower pots. I was *really* frightened then! I turned to my buddies and said, "Do y'all see that head?" They said, "Yeah, we do!" I said, "What are we going to do?" We were talking very softly. Dopey Jordan said loud enough so whoever was on the porch could hear it, "I'll get me a rock, and we'll find out who's up there!" When he said that, they heard him.

All of a sudden, these two people stood up on our front porch, and I heard a voice say, "Charles?" I realized it must be somebody that knew me, and I didn't recognize them. It wasn't light enough. I took a few steps closer to the house so I could see who it was. It was my Aunt Effie and her daughter-in-law, surprising us with a visit. Aunt Effie was my mother's brother's wife. I was so frightened they had a hard time convincing me who they were. But finally, with their help, I figured it all out.

The interesting thing was, they were not hitting the screen with their hand. They were not even around the house when all that was going on with me. I walked around to where the kitchen windows were, and there was a piece of newspaper that had blown up from somewhere, and it was lodged in the shrubbery. Obviously, when the breeze was blowing, it was flapping it against the screen. It made a sound, and when I looked over that way, it looked like it could be a person's hand hitting the screen, but it wasn't. It was that piece of newspaper just flapping in the wind.

Not long after that, Mama and Daddy came home, and I was able to tell them all that had happened. They were glad to see Aunt Effie and her daughter-in-law. If I had known they were coming, I wouldn't have been afraid, I don't think. I would have thought it was them making the noises, having fun scaring me. But Mama and Daddy didn't know they were coming.

One of the things the bigger boys who lived on the Aragon Mill village enjoyed several times during the year was playing marbles. The streets in the village were not paved, but we had curbs and sidewalks. The street itself was a dirt street. These curbs were a little more than 15 feet apart, making that the width of the dirt road. The big boys would get really serious about shooting marbles, and they drew a circle in the road, touching the curbs on both sides. In the middle of the ring they would put their marbles they were going to try to knock out with their "toy." It was amazing what they learned to do by using a ball bearing that you would get from a piece of machinery; it was just the right size. They would use that as a "toy" to shoot the marbles and knock them out of the ring.

Ulyss Jones was probably the best marble shooter that ever lived. You had to have your hand on the ring that was drawn in the dirt before you could shoot and knock marbles out. He would shoot from the ring, and it seemed the toy would go through the air almost to the pile of marbles and hit it in such a way that it would knock some out. As long as you were knocking marbles out, you could keep on shooting. Many times, he would almost clean up the circle by shooting. He had an ulterior motive for doing this. He was also the one mentioned that was such a crack shot with a slingshot. He would play for keeps, and all the marbles he kept he put into a bag. His mother saved 25-pound flour sacks, and he would put the marbles he had won in these bags.

There were times he would have a couple of those sacks full of marbles. That's when he became the "hunter with his slingshot". A marble made such a good trajectory because it was round and just the right size, and he would use that to shoot in his slingshot. All the time that he was a boy and then a young man, he had a slingshot. In those days, automobile tire tubes were made out of real rubber, and boys would get those and cut them into two strips for making slingshots. That's the kind we had at Grandma and Papa Ledford's. The prongs were made out of dogwood trees. You would find a fork in the tree limbs and cut them out to make beautiful slingshot prongs.

All the years spent living at 84 Frayser Street were good times for us boys. We grew into young men there and made many lasting memories. These memories have become good stories which I have shared with friends, grandchildren, and now great-grandchildren. I hope they enjoy hearing these stories as much as I enjoy remembering them.

The Crocker home at
84 Frayser Street

Charles as a "Marine Junior"

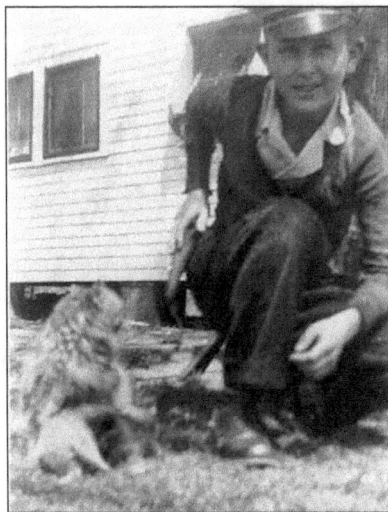

"Marine Junior" Charles with
Tabby the cat and her kittens

Aunt Venice and Uncle Roy
adored their nephews

Dean and Charles
with their puppy, Tippy

The boys at Aunt Venice's home
in Forks of Ivy, NC. Venice's dog
Trixie stands guard close by.

6

Boy Scouts

Dean and I not only joined the church at the same time, but we also joined Boy Scouts together. Scout Troop 31 was sponsored by Northside Baptist Church, and it drew boys from the Aragon mill village and the Industrial Mill. When Daddy built the addition on to Northside Church, they included a room just for Scout materials and supplies.

The mill company built a Scout cabin over in that cow pasture I've mentioned already. It wasn't a log cabin, but it was nice, with a rock fireplace. Our Scout meetings were on Monday evenings in that cabin. Later on we had our meetings at Northside Church. We couldn't keep anything in the cabin because people would break into the cabin and steal our stuff.

We would do necessary things to work on ranks—handiwork, and all kind of things like that—but at the end of Scout meeting, we also had recreation. It was always after dark when we got to that point in our Scout meeting. We would go outside and play Cops and Robbers, and all kinds of things where we had to run like crazy around that pasture.

One time Lee Faile and another boy were afraid of getting caught in our game we were playing, and they were running as hard as they could run. It was dark. One of the boys said to Lee, "we gotta remember there are bamboo bushes in this pasture!" Lee said, "Oh, I know where every one of 'em is!"

About that time, he ran right into a bamboo thorn bush. He immediately said, "There's one of them, right there!" It cut him up a little bit, but it didn't hurt him very much.

We also went Snipe Hunting for the new Scouts that were coming in to our troop. We would tell them a bunch of us were going to scare the snipes. We'd take those guys to a certain place to hold a sack, and we were going to scare the snipes into the snack. They would ask, "What are snipes?" "Well, you'll find out," we answered. We'd take them to a certain place and tell them to stand there with that tow sack open so they could catch some snipes. We'd go the other way and just keep going and leave the poor boys standing there by themselves. That was kind of mean, wasn't it? That was more of an initiation than anything else.

The Scout Oath is "On my honor, I will do my best to do my duty to God and to my country, to obey the Scout Law, to help other people at all times, to keep myself physically strong, mentally awake, and morally straight."

"A Scout is trustworthy, loyal, helpful, friendly, courteous, kind, obedient, cheerful, thrifty, brave, clean and reverent." That's the Scout Law.

After about one year in Scouts, I became Patrol Leader of the Fox Patrol. The troop was divided up into about three or four patrols, and each patrol had about seven or eight boys. One scout would be Patrol Leader of each group. Mine was the Fox Patrol. Carlton Bell was leader of the Beaver Patrol. We also had Wolf Patrol. Boys joined different patrols according to where they lived in the area. This was really good experience for me, in that at a very early age, I was learning how to work with people, getting them to do what I felt like we all needed to do. I am certain this meant a lot to me when I became a minister of music, working with choir members.

When I was Patrol Leader, we had Camporees. We'd go outside of Rock Hill somewhere, wherever we could get permission to set up camp. When we went to Camporees, we'd go on a Friday night after school, and it would always be in the spring. We'd go camp that night and through Saturday afternoon, then go home. All the patrols and troops in the Catawba District came together to camp, and we had competitions, such as Best Campsite, etc. We also had campfires and had to do demonstrations, skits, and things like that. We were learning through all these activities.

Paul Boone was Fox Patrol Leader when I joined Scouts. He was Preacher Boone's son. He was going to really fix our camp up nicely. He had a box of salt, and I think he wrote the name of his patrol, "Fox" on the ground with the salt. He got graded down for that. He didn't win the competition. Salt was not all that valuable, but this was wasteful.

Being Patrol Leader meant an awful lot to me later on, having the responsibility of being in charge of those 8 or 10 boys. Whenever we'd have a camporee, I would plan the menu. I would sit down and plan the menu for every meal, we'd split up the list, and the boys would bring certain items, then we'd put it all together. Nobody told me to do it that way. I kept that menu for supper on Friday, breakfast on Saturday, the noon meal on Saturday, and supper on Saturday, and we would eat accordingly.

When we started beautifying our campsite, I'd tell certain ones to go gather rocks. For a while, our patrol had a separate tent for a mess hall. We had a table in there, and the guys who were in charge of the whole camporee came and ate with us. We slept in an eight-man Marine tent, the same tent that was used in World Wars I and II. They were round, about the diameter of a room in your house, with a pole in the center. There was a hole in the center, and a canvas thing over the hole to close it up. You could have a fire in it, just like a teepee. For a while, when we'd go on those camporees, we'd go to Kings Mountain Battleground State Park, and we would be there with the whole council. That's where we'd have the competitions we tried to win.

We used rocks to outline our walkways from the tent to the latrine and the mess hall. We gathered enough moss to go around the rocks. The guy coming around to judge said, "This is not a camporee, this looks like a Hollywood cottage!"

I had the idea to start a fire with flint and steel, not rubbing sticks together. You had to have charred cloth to do that. We put our charred cloth in a jar to keep it from getting wet or damp. We'd put some of that cloth with some shredded burlap, take a flat rock and the flint. The sparks would ignite that cloth. You had to blow it a little, then the burlap would catch, and next thing you know, you had a fire.

We had already won the most scores in the competition— I'm talking about out of 25 or 30 patrols. We had the highest score, and the Demonstration was going to turn it. The charred cloth got damp anyway. Maybe the jar had sweated on the inside. We couldn't get that thing started to save our lives, so we didn't win.

When we went to Camp Saluda, it was for a week of camp, and we were passing merit badges like swimming, and all. We rode up there in a big ol' truck owned by a black man. The whole troop, whoever wanted to go, rode in the back of that truck. Z. N. Morrow drove his RC Cola pick-up truck up there and picked us up and drove us home. It was raining, and the boys who sat up behind the cab didn't get wet, because the rain missed them. The others got soaked, but you couldn't do anything about it.

That week we spent at Camp Saluda, I'll never forget. I was miserable! I was still wetting the bed at that time; I guess I was about 10 years old. It was embarrassing, but no one would make fun of me. It was rainy weather at camp, so the problem would tend to be worse. The big thing was, they nearly starved us to death. It was during the war, and there was a shortage of food. I remember Fodder Harris, a blond-headed boy who lived on the mill village. We had eaten everything on the table, which wasn't all that much. We had one little box of cereal at breakfast, with milk. Fodder tore up his cereal box and poured milk on it and ate it! I said, "Fodder, you're not going to eat that?!" And he said, "Yes, I am! I'm so hungry I don't know what to do!"

I've still got a dagger or knife I bought for about fifty cents at the Commissary. The handle was made out of stacks of leather. Dean bought one too. We both had one, and wearing that thing on our hip, we thought we were something!

Camp Saluda still exists, but it's called Camp Bob Hardin now. It is still the Palmetto Council camp. I could go right to it today, I guarantee you. We used to go hunting down there in that area much later.

There was something special about boys in uniform during World War II. The Boy Scouts program grew really strong because of it. They were called on to do things, besides being patriotic, to help win the war. Now, we didn't go fight, of course. There were people who were in charge of gathering newspapers in Rock Hill; certain people gathered them on certain days. People set out rolled up newspapers on Saturdays. Someone donated a big truck that was driven around town and they needed volunteers to gather the newspapers.

One weekend our troop was having a camporee in the woods at the Country Club. Whoever was in charge of getting those papers up came and asked if there were some boys who'd help to gather them. We rode on the back of that truck, jumped off at each house, picked up the newspapers, and put them in the back of the truck. This was another thing that got the Scouts got involved in helping out with the war. The newspapers were collected and recycled, and money was paid to whoever collected them. That money was then used to buy war bonds, which helped to financially support the war efforts.

When Dean and I were in Scouts, one of the badges we had to pass or earn was a 14-mile hike, in order to become Second Class Scout. We had it measured from Rock Hill to the new power dam, out there close to Ebenezer Park, that it was seven miles one way. We hiked out there and back, and that was 14 miles. We always took pork and beans with us. We opened a can of pork and beans with a Scout knife, and it made a good meal that would stay with you.

Dean said, "Charles, we gotta' eat these pork and beans fast." I said, "Why?"

He said, "Because if we eat these beans out of these cans, and we don't get them eaten up in a hurry, we'll get ptomaine poisoning." I said, "Well, that sounds serious, but it doesn't bother me at all because I'm hungry!"

We opened those cans of pork and beans (we each had a can). Boy, I started eating those things, and I got them down before you could say "jackrabbit", like it was going to kill us if we didn't eat them in about a minute. Ptomaine is food poisoning, and it'll kill you.

Dean and I went all the way through the Scout ranks together. One year at Camp, when they were presenting badges, the leader asked, "Which one of you got Tenderfoot rank first?" and we said, "We got them together."

"Well, which one of you got Second Class rank first?"

"Together."

"Well who got First Class first?"

"Together."

By that time, when he'd ask the next question, the whole troop would answer, "Together!" All the way up, (we must have been getting our Life badge at this time) it was "together." He was just having fun with the presentation. There was one person over the whole district—a man by the name of Mr. Chase was over the whole Palmetto Council at that time.

We also received our Eagle at the same time. We had to have passed the requirements for 21 merit badges. Some of those merit badges were required, and some were elective, like in school. They were for everything, like swimming for example. We had to pass a 100-yard swim. You had to pass five of them for Star Scout. There were about six or seven, or maybe 10, for Life, then the rest you had to have for Eagle. They covered marksmanship—we had .22 rifles at Boy Scout Camp in Saluda. Whenever you got ready to pass a rank or pass a merit badge, there was a Board of Review. Some adult would ask us questions for us to pass that rank.

To do Order of the Arrow, there was a stiff requirement. I never did work on Order of the Arrow. We didn't have to do an individual project like boys have to now for Eagle.

I think there were five of us in Troop 31 that got our Eagle at the same time. The Court of Honor was where the Eagle was awarded. There was a special picture made at Brownie Studio of each of the Eagle Scouts that year. Since Dean and I were brothers, we were photographed together. You'll notice when you look at that picture that it looks like Dean earned more badges than I did, but that's not so. It so happened that when we got our merit badge sashes at the local Boy Scout supply store, there weren't two the same width. Mine was a narrow sash and Dean's was wider. We both earned the same number of badges, but when Mama sewed them on the front of each sash, it looked like Dean earned more badges since his sash was wider.

When Dean and I got our Eagle Scout, they gave the whole morning service to that ceremony at Northside. Z. N. Morrow spoke that morning at the church. The mothers were called out of the congregation to pin the awards on us. After all, there were five of us getting our Eagle badges at the same time. I was 14 years old. You couldn't be in Scouts under the age of 12. We had Cub Scouts back then too, and there was Girl Scouts.

There was also the Bessie Peacock Award. She was my sixth grade school teacher at Northside Elementary. She took it upon herself to give a medal, kind of like the Olympic medals you see today. It had a ribbon with it. I think the Troop had a part in voting, and I think the Scout Master had a lot to do with choosing who would receive it. She gave it to the boy who tried the hardest to be a good Scout, being friendly to the other scouts, etc. I received it one year.

I got two ranks above Eagle, but Dean only got one. There were three palms—a palm branch pin that was pinned on the ribbon part of the Eagle badge. The first palm was bronze, then silver and gold. You had to pass above the 21 merit badges for Eagle. You had to pass five more to get bronze, an additional five to get the next one, then an additional five to get the third one. I got 10 merit badges above Eagle, and that enabled me to pass the silver level. There weren't names for those levels.

We were in Sea Scouts for a while. That didn't materialize, really. We were already getting older and losing interest in scouting. We went down to Jacksonville Naval Air Base in Florida. I got really seasick, and I wasn't the only one. We rode on a destroyer escort. I thought it was a big ship, because all I'd seen was boats on the backwater. Man, that thing was longer than a house! But that was just a ship that was used to escort destroyers in the Navy during the war.

You won't believe how hard I worked to get rid of the problem I had with my lips! We were down close to the Equator, and out on the deck of that ship, my lips got parched, and they cracked and got infected. We were out there about two weeks. When we got back to land, my lips started getting infected, and I got permission to go to a drug store. I got me some Dr. Porter's Antiseptic Healing Oil. I kept a bottle of that stuff in my pocket, because it was getting close to time to go home. I was going to be seeing Mae, so I kept my lips greasy from that stuff to get them to heal faster!

We got back to Rock Hill in the middle of the night, and the bus driver of that Greyhound bus offered to take each one of us home to where we lived for about a dollar. He delivered us right to our homes. When Mama saw me, she said, "Charles, what in the world is wrong?" I told her what had happened. Mr. Mullis was talking to Mama and Daddy and the church about it, and they told him what had happened (he wasn't with us on the trip), and that I'd put Dr. Porter's Antiseptic Healing Oil on it. Mr. Mullis said there probably wasn't a better thing I could have done. That was some of the most potent stuff for healing that you've ever seen in your life! It mainly had camphor in it. I was wanting to kiss Mae as soon as I saw her!

Dean was never a Patrol Leader. When he was older, and about the time he passed his Eagle Scout, he became Assistant Scout Master. Soon, Dean was old enough to join the Navy, and the Korean War was going on. He joined the Navy before receiving the Palms. He later came back, after he got out of service, and worked with Mr. Mullis and the Scout Troop. He passed all the way up to Scout Master Key; the highest you could go.

I will always believe that my experience in Scouts trained me for many things I would face later on in life, such as working with volunteers and leading others. I had good leaders, and a lot of opportunities to grow in many ways. Looking back now, many years later, I am really thankful for the whole Scouting experience.

Charles and Dean earned their Eagle Award in Scouts at the same time

Charles' Eagle pin with the bronze and silver palms
signifying ten merit badges above Eagle

Sea Scouts (Charles is fourth from the left)

7

Church Music:
The Beginning

You remember my earlier story of Mrs. Robinson and the "tom" cat she gave me that turned out to be a female cat. She also happened to be my Junior Choir leader, the choir that I sang in as a child at Northside Baptist Church. There's a story behind Mrs. Robinson and the Junior Choir.

My dad, L. F. Crocker, was the choir director at Northside Baptist Church when I was a child and for years after I became an adult. We were like most churches in those days that had only an adult choir. That choir wasn't necessarily doing anything serious in choral music, but they were practicing on Wednesday nights and having what we called "special music" on Sunday, and that was about it.

One year, Dad went to Ridgecrest for Music Week. It was there that Dr. B. B. McKinney introduced the "graded choir program," meaning a choir for different ages, including children and all the way through adults. They promoted having this kind of arrangement of graded choirs in the church. There was a choir for the Cradle Roll, they called it, the Beginner Choir, the Primary Choir, and the Junior Choir. These were the different age levels. I was a member in that Junior Choir level, and Mrs. Robinson was the leader.

Dad came back home from Ridgecrest all excited after hearing B. B. McKinney introduce this graded choir program, and it wasn't any time before we had the choirs I've already mentioned, a full graded choir program. It meant an awful lot to Northside Baptist Church. I remember having a lot of music at Northside, with all the choirs, but it was not a serious matter until Daddy organized the graded choir program.

I remember singing a duet with Peggy Farrell at age eight. This was part of a program we were doing in the old church, across the railroad from where it is now, the church in which I accepted Christ and was baptized. I sang solos in church when I wasn't but nine years old. I'm not trying to impress anybody; I'm just saying I've always loved music and participating in it. It started at a very early age, with my dad, at Northside Baptist.

When I mention Dad being the choir director, you need to know that he was not a minister of music paid to do so. He gave his time like he had by helping to build the church and wire the church, draw the plans for a large building, and a lot of things like that which he enjoyed doing, using his God-given talents in so many different ways. The interest in music was passed from him on to me because I have always made it known that I enjoy music. Music has always been a part of my life.

Dad was not satisfied to just rehearse something out of the hymn book on Wednesday and have the choir sing it on Sunday. He was determined to stretch the choir, to take them to greater heights in music, which I always admired in him. He was determined that they were going to learn the *Hallelujah Chorus* from Handel's *Messiah*. The *Hallelujah Chorus* happened to be in the back of the Broadman Hymnal, and believe it or not, it was in shaped notes ("shape" meaning do, re, me, fa, so, la, ti, do; a different shape for each note of the scale). The lady who played the piano said she would not have time to give to learning the *Hallelujah Chorus*, but she made it very clear that when it came time to sing it, she was expecting to be the one to accompany.

Believe it or not, my dad taught Northside Baptist Church Choir the *Hallelujah Chorus* without an accompanist! He just about drove us all crazy around the house trying to get the tricky rhythms (at least they were tricky to him). He was not a highly trained musician; he was just a man with a lot of talent. He went to Andrews Music Store in Charlotte and bought the whole *Messiah* on twelve-inch, 78-rpm records to get the *Hallelujah Chorus*. That's how determined he was to make this happen. It was two volumes of about 30-something records. Even though they were 12-inch records, at 78 rpm, there wasn't room for more than one or two songs on each side.

That recording of *Messiah* became a part of my life when I was only an 11- or 12-year-old boy. I would sit in front of Dad's record player with a copy of Handel's *Messiah* in my hand. I was fascinated by it. I loved it, and all the while, wondered how in the world anybody could learn all that music. I had not even thought about why I was so fascinated by it. I would sit for hours at a time, with that score in my hand, listening.

I was really fascinated by *Comfort Ye* and *Every Valley*, the tenor solos at the beginning. I learned *Comfort Ye My People* listening to that recording and following the music. I had taken violin lessons for a few months when I was in the latter part of the fourth grade and the beginning of the fifth grade. That helped me to be able to read music just enough to follow what I was hearing off the record. Those violin lessons did not continue because Dad could not afford it. I wasn't old enough to work and make money to pay for it myself.

After learning *Comfort Ye My People*, I decided I was going to give *Every Valley* a try, not realizing that no one picks that piece of music up and is able to sing it without an awful lot of work, but it happened after I became a seminary student (which is part of my story later). I didn't know why I was so interested in music in those days, when other boys on the mill village were playing ball and doing all kinds of things that uneducated and poor people would do. I was so interested in music, and the music was great music, not just some piece of junk. All of that was revealed to me later in life, which I'll get into in the next chapters.

I would listen to *Every Valley* with the score in hand, and then I would go into a part of the house where I didn't think anybody could hear me, not realizing that singing it without accompaniment would make it doubly hard to do. Even a trained musician would find that difficult, and I was just a boy. The thing was, there was a window in that room, and Earl was out in the yard, washing the car, and I didn't know he could hear me. He enjoyed teasing me about my singing, but I knew he would support me in anything I'd want to do. He would walk up to the window, and he would say, "Charles, who in the world ever told you that you could sing?" He enjoyed teasing me when I would sing a solo on Sunday morning in church. We would gather around the dinner table, and he would say, "Well everything this morning at church was great, all but one thing." Everybody at the table knew he was making reference to my singing, however, I knew he was just teasing me. I didn't have a great voice—still don't—but I knew he was just teasing me and having fun with his brother.

I mentioned about my taking violin lessons when I was a child. After a month or two of lessons, I and two other kids, one of whom played clarinet and the other played violin, and our teacher, Miss Woodward, played a march for the kids to enter the chapel program on Fridays. Back in those days, even in elementary school, we had Chapel every Friday with some kind of a program.

Before that, when I was in the fourth grade, we had class playing the tonette, a black, hard rubber whistle-like, that had the scale on it. I played it by ear, and never really learned the fingering. There was a time set aside every week for that group to gather and have instructions on how to play the tonette. Sometimes during recess, when other kids were playing ball or some other sport, I was sitting on some concrete steps, trying to compose some tunes with my tonette. I knew just enough about the different notes to be able to put them on a staff because of my violin lessons. I didn't realize that was something I wasn't supposed to be able to do at that age without more training. I tried anyway. Again, I say this expresses my interest in music.

When I was taking violin lessons from Mr. Allen, who was the band director at Rock Hill High School, he encouraged me to go to a concert at Winthrop College Auditorium. It was a very heavy music concert, which you would expect to hear at a university, especially one that had a very fine music department like Winthrop College. I was young enough that Mama did not want me to go by myself, so she twisted Dean's arm and had him go with me. You may wonder, why such heavy music for a child so young?

When I became a teenager, I was very active in the high school chorus, male chorus and mixed chorus, under the direction of Mrs. Rosa B. Guess. At the same time, I was singing for weddings, singing solos in church, for funerals, and enjoyed doing so. I worked at Wolf-Todd-Morris Funeral Home when I was a teenager, and anytime a family had a funeral taking place at the funeral home, and they wanted someone to sing but didn't know anyone, they would ask me to do it. I think that's one of the reasons I got the job there. This made for a good arrangement for the funeral home, to have someone on staff that could do this.

George Finley was my accompanist most of the time, who happened to be the pianist for Daddy's quartet when I was a very young child. He could play any song in any key without looking at the music. This made it a lot easier for me.

What I liked most about working at the funeral home was being able to drive the ambulance once in a while. They didn't allow me to drive it when it was an emergency, but sometimes I'd be in the ambulance, going somewhere necessary and get to drive by the school, and kids would see me in the ambulance. After all, I was just a teenager, at the age I enjoyed this kind of thing.

I not only sang in the Glee Club and Mixed Chorus under Mrs. Guess, but I also represented our school singing a tenor solo at the festival at Winthrop College. Every year we had some outstanding choral conductor come to Winthrop College, and schools from all over the state of South Carolina would bring their choruses and have this person work with them on music that was going to be done at the festival in the spring. The first part of this took place in the fall. Then we rehearsed this music during the year and performed it in the spring. Mr. Harry Robert Wilson was the one that came many times from Columbia University in New York. When

I sang my solo as a part of the festival, he was judging it and making suggestions as to how to improve my singing. This was done for all the students.

An interesting thing happened when I was there at Winthrop College for festival. Mrs. Guess was warming me up in a classroom. She decided to go get Dr. Roberts, who headed up the music department at Winthrop, and brought him around to hear me sing my solo. When I sang it for him, he caught an error, a misprint in the music, just by hearing it one time, not being familiar with it at all. He pointed to the music and said, "If you sing this note, as you're seeing it, it does not harmonize with the accompaniment like it's supposed to, and you'll be graded down on it."

I thought it was interesting that Mrs. Guess decided to go get him. It made a difference in the way I sang that piece. I would have sung it as a mistake, and Harry Robert Wilson would have caught it. I think the Lord had something to do with that arrangement. Mrs. Guess became a very close friend of mine. She encouraged me to do something with my life in music. Everything seemed to point me in that direction. I had no voice lessons, other than what Mrs. Guess gave me to encourage me to do something with my voice. I'm proud to say that when I was judged in that music festival, Dr. Wilson gave me a first rating "Superior" and wrote all kinds of nice things all over the music.

To quote Walter Brennan, the movie actor, who said many times, "No brag, just fact." It was quite a coincidence that Dr. Roberts happened to be close enough by that she could call him into the practice room to hear me. I didn't think much about it at the time, but I know now why it happened.

To have this kind of encouragement in developing my interest in music made a big impact on me, and it served to make my desire to pursue a music career of some kind just that much stronger. I was surrounded by people who gave me opportunities and helped me to get the training I needed. I look back on these people with a lot of appreciation for what they did to encourage me.

Little Village Choir in Rock Hill, SC. Charles is fourth from the left, back row. His father Farrell is fourth from the right, back row.

High school

8

The Lord's Calling

A year or two after my experience at the Winthrop choral festival, I began feeling led to do something in full-time Christian work. I responded to a sermon by Rev. J. J. Boone at the old Northside Baptist, my home church. The sermon was about being called into the ministry. I made a commitment along with several other people that night. I had been saving my money for several years before that commitment, and wanted to go to Westminster Choir College. This was part of Mrs. Guess' influence.

For many years, even when I was in elementary school, John Finley Williamson, from Westminster Choir College, came to Winthrop College and worked with children from all over the state. Westminster was publicized quite a bit. The fact that he came from Westminster to Rock Hill was special, and it seemed logical for me to want to go to that school because of him. It seemed like the place to go, however you could not go very many places and study church music like you could at Westminster.

Along about these same years, I became bothered by what I was supposed to do with my life, even though I had made a commitment the night I heard Rev. Boone speak. I wasn't sure what phase of Christian work I wanted to do. I would walk down the street and see some person doing a certain kind of work. I'd stop and look, wondering, "How would I like to do that for a means of livelihood?" Then I'd say to myself, "No, I don't think I would." This happened for quite a while; it was really eating on me. I became obsessed with trying to find the answer to what I wanted to do with my life. I decided to talk to Dad about it. Dad had always been interested in what we boys were doing and wanted to advise wherever he could because of his experience in life. Before talking to Dad, I decided to open the Bible and try to find God's message to me through the scriptures. Every scripture that I came to seemed to point in the direction of doing some kind of full-time Christian work. This happened by just opening the Bible and letting my eyes fall where they may. I don't mean there was some sort of supernatural power entering into this, but I thought it was very interesting it would happen in that way.

After explaining to Dad about what was taking place in my mind, I asked him if he thought this could be God speaking to me through the scriptures I read and other things that had taken place, such as commitment on the night Rev. Boone had spoken on the subject. I still didn't know what phase I wanted to go into. Dad said he saw no reason why it could not be the Lord speaking to me and wanting me to do something for him. I'll never forget what Dad said to me: "Don't worry about what phase of full-time Christian work you're supposed to do. You just give your heart and life solely to Him, and He will not make a mistake with your life. He will put you in the right place at the right time, according to His leadership." I've heard Dad refer to this several times. He said he would never forget what happened when he told me that. He said it seemed there was a big boulder that had just rolled off my shoulders at the time we were talking.

From that day forward, I don't remember a time when I stopped and said, "Hey, I know what I want to do." It just seemed that I naturally went in the direction of music. I knew that God had instilled in me the love for music, and I enjoyed participating in it. I had already done quite a bit at such a young age. It just seemed to make sense that God was leading me in that direction. So, that's what I did. It seemed the decision was already made for me.

One of the reasons I didn't think about doing music to start with, was that there were few churches that had a full-time minister of music. It was only the large downtown churches that had a paid minister of music, but most of the time, they were part-time and had a job in a college or high school somewhere in the town, and were doing the music in the church on the side. My dad was a volunteer choir director for 15 years at Northside Baptist Church when I was growing up. About the time I left to go to the seminary, however, he had begun serving churches in the Rock Hill and York County areas, receiving some compensation for it. He worked just as hard when he was a volunteer director as he did after he became paid for it. He was just that kind of a person.

About the time I was making my decision to do church music, Dad was already thinking about retiring as a volunteer choir director at Northside. He had served the church for 15 years, and he told the pastor and deacons that it was time that he stepped aside, that he had carried the music as far as he could go with what training he'd had, and it was time the church should get a minister of music, a person trained for that position. The church took his suggestion and voted to call a full-time minister of music. In those days it was "minister of music and education." Most churches like Northside could not afford two different people, one on each of those jobs, so they were able to pay a decent salary to one person who would give time to both of those positions. They began looking for a minister of music and education, and after writing letters to the different seminaries, they found Milas MacDonnell, who was a student at Southern Seminary Music School in Louisville, Kentucky.

About this same time, Mae and I were attracted to each other and began making plans to someday marry. My plan was that I would go to school and be trained to become a minister of music. My first thought was Westminster, for reasons given earlier. To tell you the truth, I did not even know that there was such a thing as a music school at any of the seminaries. I began saving money toward that end.

It wasn't possible for a high school kid to make very much money at part-time jobs.

I got a job working at the A&P Supermarket with Lloyd Shaw, part-time. He was part of the Shaw family that became our friends when we first came to Rock Hill. He was the oldest child in that family. I recall that I sold $1,300 worth of fruit and trees around Christmastime, which was a lot of money in those days. This success got me a job inside the store, which I took, and I worked with Lloyd in the produce department. That store was next door to White's Bicycle Shop.

After working at A&P for a while, I got a job in the bicycle shop, repairing bikes. We sharpened lawn mowers and made keys. I also did something which coincides with working with bikes—I began taking bicycles home that needed a paint job, and I painted bikes, tricycles, scooters, wagons, anything people wanted painted. This was done after I had worked through the bicycle, repairing what it needed in the way of mechanical help. This kind of work led me into fixing up old bikes and selling them, especially at Christmastime. This association with the bicycle shop led me into motorbikes—Cushman motor scooters—and I did a lot of swapping and selling in that area too. It was through this that I got the reputation with the family as being a tightwad. I always had money, even though it wasn't a whole lot.

Dad borrowed money from me to buy Mama her first washing machine. Up until that time, clothes were washed out behind the house in an old wash pot and three tubs with a scrub board. One of my jobs on Monday morning, which was wash day, was to cut some kindling and build a fire under the wash pot to boil the clothes.

Earl and Dean teased me really often about my swapping, buying, and selling. Working at White's Bicycle Shop coincided with my love for riding a bicycle. This was my sport when I was a teenager. I played a little bit of football in elementary school, but I never did play the sports of that kind very much. My sport was riding a bicycle. This worked into riding long distances, such as from Rock Hill to Kings Mountain to visit kinfolk. I also entered a number of bicycle races, which they called bicycle rodeos. It happened in a football field at Northside School, and was not like riding on city streets. We did all kinds of things on a bicycle. The only time I was ever beaten was a slow race. In all the other races, the first one across the line would win. The slow race winner was the last person to cross. The idea was to keep the bicycle balanced and not have to put your foot down. If you put your foot down, you were disqualified. There was a boy named Bobby Sweat who had perfected this business riding out just a few feet, and he just stopped, completely balanced, without kicking the stand down. He would balance that bicycle; he turned it just a little bit to the side. He could just stand there without putting his foot down. I never did really learn to do that. When I got on a bicycle, I wanted to *go* and not stand around! He won that race. The prizes were things like a basket for my bicycle, maybe a headlight or a taillight. I won every fast race and had a lot of fun doing it.

There was a very interesting trip that I wanted to take with my buddy, Jerry Buchanan (pronounced Buck-hannon). We were the same age, and we hit it off there on the mill village. His father and his brother worked at the Aragon Mill. We got to know each other well. His father said one of the nicest things that has ever been said about me, and I'll never forget it. When Jerry would say, "I want to go here or there with Charles Crocker," his dad said, "Son, you can go anywhere you want to go, as long as you're with Charles Crocker." And that's no brag; that's just fact.

Jerry was into biking a good bit, too. I was riding a fairly new Columbia, which was the bicycle sold at White's Bicycle Shop, where I worked. Jerry had a good bicycle, but it wasn't new. We planned a trip, to go somewhere far enough away that we would feel like we had really done something. I said, "Let's go to King's Mountain, and we'll go to my grandmother's and step-granddaddy's." By this time Grandma and Papa Ledford had already sold their farm at Carpenter's Knob, which I mentioned earlier, and had gone to King's Mountain, where they knew more people and had more protection. They weren't doing nearly as much farming. So Jerry and I set a date to get on our bikes and head towards King's Mountain. We called Grandma Ledford to make sure they were going to be at home, of course, and we took off. We were not trying to have a race or anything like that. We were just enjoying what we were doing, pedaling along. We had both biked enough that we could talk as we rode, and not be all out of breath. We just had a big time.

We got above York and stopped at a cotton gin that was in progress. It was at the intersection of the highway that goes to Clover and the other highway leading to King's Mountain. We stopped there in that crossroad. We had never seen a cotton gin working. I had always thought that would be interesting. We asked questions, and they let us go right where the cotton was being ginned. A cotton gin was a very large machine that they ran the cotton through, and it would take the seeds out of the cotton. A boll of cotton was intertwined with the seed in such a way that if you picked it out by hand, it would take forever. Eli Whitney, if you remember, invented the cotton gin that made it possible for farmers to take their cotton and run it through that machine. The seeds went out one way for cow feed, and the cotton went another direction.

We enjoyed learning about that, and then got back on our bikes and went on toward King's Mountain. It was still about 15 to 18 miles to Grandma's house, because we had to go into King's Mountain and then go west for several miles. From Rock Hill to their house was probably about 40 miles. Dean and I had made a trip to Uncle Luther's, who lived out in the country on the south side of King's Mountain, but it was only 32 miles there.

We went on up the road and out west to Grandma's and Papa's. She was expecting us for lunch, and we got there in time. She had a big meal, and we really enjoyed it. It so happened that Jerry had some cousins in Shelby. From King's Mountain to Shelby was about 11 miles, but he had to ride back into King's Mountain from Grandma's house to take the road to Shelby, which he did. He borrowed my bicycle because it was a new bike. We may have had to adjust the seat a little bit, but we got it ready, and he took off on my bike. I piddled around the house there, and talked to Papa and listened to his stories. I said, "Papa, do you have any dove around?" This was dove season, and even though I was in North Carolina and didn't have a North Carolina license, I said, "When Jerry gets back, I would like to borrow your shotgun and see if we can get us a dove or two." He said, "I'll be happy to let you use my gun." He had a really good double-barrel shotgun, and he had the kind of shells we needed to shoot dove, a #8 shot for bird. I piddled around and probably took a nap because I was tired after riding all the way up there.

Later on that afternoon, Jerry came riding up, and we talked a little bit. I said, "Papa's going to let me have his shotgun. Do you want to go down here in the edge of the woods and see if we can kill us a dove or two?" He said, "Yeah, let's do that."

We got the shotgun, went down to the woods and walked around. I don't remember how many dove came over, if any, but I do remember walking up on a snake. It was in the fall of the year and already getting colder, but it happened to be warmer that day. A big ol' coach whip snake was coiled up in the sun because it was warmer. I said, "*Good night*, Jerry, looky there!" I've always been afraid of snakes. They just give me the heebie-jeebies. I backed up and took that shotgun, and I killed that snake. The shot hit him in such a way that it cut him into about four or five different pieces, just squirming all over the ground. The bad thing that happened was that when I fired that barrel, the first barrel, I dropped the muzzle down toward the ground, and then the second barrel fired even though I didn't pull the trigger. It just fired on its own. It scared the daylights out of me, and Jerry too. I said, "Jerry, I'm glad I learned gun safety in Scouts, because I was holding that gun exactly in the position I should have, and that shot went right in the ground and we didn't get hurt." It almost kicked the gun right out of my hand. I immediately thought about the time we were at Carpenter's Knob and there were some crows in the corn field down a ways from the house, and Papa brought that shotgun out to scare the crows out of the corn field. When he fired the first barrel, the second barrel fired too. I remembered that, although I was a much younger boy at the time.

When we got back to the house, I told Papa what had happened. He said, "Well, let's look at that shotgun." A double-barrel shotgun, when it's breached down to put shells in it, is cocked once it's closed, and it's ready to shoot again as soon as you put shells in it. We made sure it did not have a shell in it. He cocked it, he breached the gun and cocked it. He pulled one trigger and the second trigger went off by itself. He said, "Oh, I'll have this fixed." I said, "Well, I hope you will! It's too dangerous for you to be shooting that thing!" It seemed like it was a long time between the time he fired that gun in the corn fields to scare those crows and the time we were talking then, but as I've thought about it, it wasn't but about two or three years.

Well, Jerry and I messed around and rested a while. It wasn't late enough for supper, but Grandma had a snack for us, and we drank some water and got back on our bikes to head home. It was late enough, and the days were already shorter, that we started out not too long before dark. We had lights on our bicycles, and there wasn't a lot of traffic in those days, not on that highway, not like today. It didn't seem to be too dangerous, and we needed to get back to Rock Hill before too late. We had about 40 miles to go. We went up to King's Mountain and got back on Highway 161 and headed toward Rock Hill.

An interesting thing happened. It was a little later than dusk dark; it was late enough that we had our lights on. We happened to look over to our right, over in the west, and there was either a barn or a house or both that was on fire. It was late enough that we could see the blaze from that fire very clearly. We wondered what in the world was going on and hoped it wasn't somebody's house. We stopped there for a minute and watched the fire. We got back on our bikes, still talking, and we could still see the burning house or barn. We were riding along and Jerry was looking at the house. He happened to get close enough with his front wheel to my back wheel axle (the axle on a bicycle back then stuck out just a little bit) just long enough for it to hit the spokes in his front wheel. When he did that, he ripped out about three spokes from his wheel. It didn't hurt mine at all. The thing is, they were right together. I'd worked on bicycles enough to know that if you didn't have a spoke wrench, you were in trouble. That wheel was warped to the point that it was rubbing the fork. The fork is the part of the metal that comes down on each side of the front wheel, and that's the way you steer it, of course. It was hard to peddle and we were still way above York. It was almost like riding with the brakes on.

I said, "Well, Jerry, you ride a ways, then I'll ride it a ways and you can ride my bike." He said, "Man, that's a deal!" We did that, got into York, and on down to the other side of York. Earl was coming up the road in his car, and he saw us. I don't remember where he was going, but he pulled over and stopped. He said, "What in this world are y'all doing up here?" I told him what we had done and where we'd been, and I said, "We're in trouble because we can't ride this thing too well with it rubbing the fork like that." Wherever Earl was going, he couldn't put the bikes in the car and give us a ride home. I had hoped he could, but he couldn't, so we had to tough it out. We were going down Fishing Creek hill fast enough that with that tire rubbing the fork, it got almost red hot. The tire was smoking, and I don't know what kept the tire from blowing, but it didn't. I guess the Lord had something to do with that. We toughed it out, and we got to Rock Hill. Jerry had ridden the bike more than I did, and he was just about to pass out, he was so tired. We got in the house at Mama and Daddy's. He didn't even go on home right then. He got over in the corner behind the heater, where it was really good and warm, and the next thing I knew he was sound asleep! That was the good ol' days.

Another story that includes Jerry Buchanan took place when we were each about 14 years old. I've already mentioned the fact that the people on the mill village were allowed to have livestock, such as cows, pigs, etc. Jerry and I decided we were going to try to raise a pig. It so happened that Jerry had an uncle who was a farmer and raised livestock, of course, and lived between Rock Hill and Charlotte. He had an old sow hog that was pregnant with Lord-only-knows-how-many pigs. They usually had six or eight piglets in one breeding. We decided we wanted to talk to him about getting a pig apiece from him in order to raise them.

We got on my Cushman motor scooter and rode over to Jerry's uncle's farm to talk with him about getting a pig from him. We were going to try to pay him for the pigs, but he said, "No, I won't sell you a pig, but I'll make a deal with you." We said, "What's that?" He said, "I'll let each of you earn a pig." So we immediately asked how in the world this could happen. He said, "I have some terraces, down across the highway there on the lower part of my farm, that need cleaning off." A terrace is the way the land is piled up in a row in such a way that it will hold the water and keep the dirt from washing away. It makes for better bottom land that would have more water for growth. He said, "If you boys will clean those terraces off, get all that brush and grass and whatever else is on the terrace off, I'll give each of you a pig." We said, "Boy, that's a deal!" We didn't have any money to buy a pig anyway.

So we set a date that we would go back to his uncle's farm and later began our work earning a pig apiece. We took along a few tools that we might need and managed to get back over there on my Cushman motor scooter, one of us holding the tools and the other one driving and guiding the scooter.

It so happened this was being done the time of year there were wasps all around the bushes and small trees we were trying to clear off the terraces. We found wasp nests we didn't know about. We started cutting small trees and bushes, and all of a sudden, we both got stung. After doing that, we looked ahead, and we could see other nests on down the terrace. I said, "Jerry, there's not but one way to do this, looks to me like, and that is to burn the growth that we're trying to cut out, and at the same time, we'll get the wasp nests, and won't get stung again."

We both decided that sounded like a winner. We got a large can and one of us went back to a service station and got about two gallons of gas. Now, in those days, that was not all that wasteful because gas was about twenty cents a gallon! Wouldn't that be nice now, in the 2012 era?

We got back with the gas, and we would take a quart can, fill it with gas, then pour it out along the terrace and light a match to it. I don't recommend this for anybody to do, especially young people like we were. It was extremely dangerous because we could have had just enough gasoline on our clothing and hands that it could have ignited and burned us both very seriously. But it sure did work on getting rid of the wasps. We would light the fire and let it burn down. What little bit was left we would put out, and then we would cut the small trees and brush. The only problem was, there were several terraces, and we weren't making much progress with that one terrace, so we decided that was going to be too hard to do. We also thought that Jerry's uncle would feel sorry for us and say "Well, you guys have earned a pig anyway."

So we went back to him after we had done about half the job and asked him if he would come through with giving us a pig anyway or at least selling us one at a reduced cost. He taught us a lesson. He said, "No, our agreement was that you boys would clean those terraces off, and I would give you a pig apiece. You haven't finished your job, and I'm not going to give you a pig. Now, if you want to keep working and *earn* the pigs, I'll agree to that, but not until you do."

Well, we learned a very important lesson that you've got to keep your word when you have an agreement with someone like that. Needless to say, we did not get into the hog raising business. We went back home empty-handed, except for the tools we carried over there.

I'll never forget the first time I laid eyes on Mae. We happened to have Homeroom together in high school. She had finished the eighth grade as part of her schooling at Central. I went to high school from the seventh grade at Northside School, and we ended up in the ninth grade in the same homeroom. We went to Homeroom at the start of each day. The roll was checked, and shortly thereafter, the bell would ring, and we would go to our first period class.

I had never seen Mae until the first time our homeroom gathered that year. At that time she was sitting a little toward the back of the room, or at least she had a need to go up and ask the teacher something, and she walked by my desk, not knowing me at all, and I did not know her. I remember looking at her and thinking what a beautiful girl she was. It's very interesting that she was very dark skinned, so with her dark brown hair and the color of her skin, I thought she was what we call Latino today. Buddy Hawkins, another good buddy of mine, was sitting next to me, and he called to my attention how beautiful she was, and I agreed with him.

There wasn't much time during homeroom period to do much talking with one another, but it so happened that Mae and I had science class together. We were sitting in such a way that with a subdued whisper, we could talk with one another, and we became acquainted. Later in the year, I was having a little trouble understanding part of what we were studying, and she offered for me to come to her house so we could study together. We were studying for a test. I made an A on that test. I sure was glad she offered to study together, because I wanted to get to know her a little better anyway!

As the school year went on, her dark suntan began to "fade" but that didn't keep me from being interested in her. I guess I realized by then that she wasn't Latino at all. I learned later that she had spent the whole summer at Myrtle Beach with her mother, and that's why she had such a dark tan. We continued to have study times together, and that meant a lot to me and helped me in what we were studying.

Mae and I began "going together." We were members of the Bible Club in high school. You don't have this kind of thing much anymore, but in those days, you could take a Bible class. It was taught by Loretta Trumble. One year Mae was President of the Bible class, and you'll never guess what my job was with that class. You guessed it! I was the music director.

One of the things Mae led the Bible class to do was to gather food from friends and relatives and take it to poor people who were hungry. I remember one time, it was close to Christmas, and I said, let's gather some food and take it to one of the places where we had helped before, that we knew needed help in that way. We went to Mama and Daddy, Venice and Roy, and gathered quite a bit of food. A few of our neighbors pitched in on it. We took it over beyond Fort

Mill, SC, where we'd gone before. We got to the house and no one was at home, but the door was open. Back in those days, people didn't lock their doors like they do now. We opened the door, went in, and set quite a sizeable amount of food on their kitchen table, and left. To this day, they don't know who in the world did it. We received a lot of joy in doing that.

Needless to say, Mae's and my relationship developed into more than just meeting at her house to study science or whatever. We actually fell in love as much as anybody could, and with our parents' consent, decided to marry. We dated more than two years before marriage, which is to say it was not just a little fling that might not work out. We decided to get married, which we did the night before Easter Sunday, 1949.

People might say we didn't know what love was about at that young age. My Uncle Deck, as much as I thought of him and believed he was a really fine man, he would say to me, "Charles, you don't know what love is." I don't know what understanding love has to do with age. I had sweethearts all my life, but I didn't really fall in love until Mae. She has always stood by me in hard times, with the proper encouragement to go on and do something with my life. I have thanked the Lord for this beautiful relationship ever since we married.

At the time this autobiography is being written, we have celebrated our 63rd wedding anniversary! I think if we stay together another year or two, we'll be able to make this thing work!

Getting married at 17 years old seems awfully early in life to some people, but it was a very common thing in those days. There were a number of married couples going to Rock Hill High School. I think one of the reasons for this was that not nearly as many people went off to college back then, as they do these days. You have to remember this was also the tail end of the Great Depression, and money was not as free to get further education.

Because of the money situation, I was going to work for a while, and Mae was going to work to help with finances, however, we were blessed with the coming of our son David.

We decided to postpone any thoughts of going off to school until a later date. We didn't have any specific time set anyway, and we thought this would be the way to go.

I got a job at the Aragon Mill, in the slasher room, and Mae went to work at the Victoria Mill in Rock Hill. She worked in the cloth room. She was on the first shift, which was from seven to three, and I was on the second shift, from 4:00 until midnight. I took care of David during the daytime, and she cared for him beginning at 4:00 in the afternoon. Boy did we make a lot of money! I was making about a dollar an hour, and so was she. My paycheck, with Social Security taken out, was 38 dollars-and-something for a week's work of 40 hours. She had about the same amount. Would you say that things have changed greatly?

While I was working at the Aragon Mill, Donna, our second child, was born. I came home from work at midnight, and started to get ready for bed. Mae saw that I was getting ready to go to bed, and she said, "you'd better not come to bed yet; I feel like I may be starting the first stages of labor." Donna was born about 6:00 the next morning.

Back in those days, the school system would arrange for a person to take subjects during the morning hours to complete a high school diploma, so they could work in the mill in the late afternoon and evening. There were about 15 mills in Rock Hill at that time, and most everybody earned a living in textiles. I had that kind of arrangement with school by going to class during the morning hours, with my mother taking care of David.

Now back to Milas MacDonnell. Milas had several years of formal music training in college and at Southern Seminary Church Music Department. He had been trained to be a minister of music in a church, and this got my attention. As I mentioned earlier, I had experienced singing in the children's choirs while growing up, which Dad started years before. I had not really sung in the adult choir too awfully long. Someone told Milas MacDonnell that I sang solos, and he asked me to sing for him, which I did. He gave me a solo to learn; it was one that I had already been interested in as a boy—"Comfort Ye My People" from Handel's *Messiah*. After I sang this in a service, he began encouraging me to go further my voice and get some training. He felt that I had something to offer in this way. He said, "Charles, have you ever thought about going on to school, and becoming a minister of music?" I said, "Yes, I have thought about this, but I don't see how on earth I can pay tuition until I can work some more years to save some money." He looked at me and said, "What tuition?" I said, "Well, I would have to pay tuition to go to school. They don't let you do that for nothing." He said the place I'm thinking about your going, there is no tuition." I said, "I find that hard to believe. Where is that?" He said, "The Church Music Department of Southern Seminary, in Louisville, Kentucky." I was really shocked and surprised to learn that I could go to school and learn to be a minister of music without tuition. He said, "Your tuition is paid under the auspices of the Southern Baptist Convention. You will only have a few small fees to pay each semester, but that is not considered tuition as you were thinking of it."

I went home and immediately talked to Mae. "Do you know what I just learned?" Of course she said, "What?" I told her about my conversation with Milas MacDonell, and when I got to the part where he said there was no tuition, but we'd have to have a place to live and all if we were going to do this, she said, "That's very interesting because I was just reading the *Baptist Courier* (which was the state Baptist paper) "and learned that Southern Baptists have just purchased a very large apartment complex to make room for seminary students to go there and live and study."

This whole idea came up in our conversations for the next few days and weeks. I finally said, "Do you think we can do this?" She said, "Of course I do!" I said, "Well, let's look into it further and see what we can work out." I went back to Milas MacDonnell and asked about the fact that I did not have any college training, and I thought I would have to have a college degree before I could go to the seminary. He immediately said, "That's not true, because what you would be getting is a diploma in sacred music. It is not a degree, but it would equip you to be a successful minister of music in a church if you wanted to be." That made it even more attractive to think about doing this.

I went to him very often over the next few weeks, asking all kinds of questions about the idea of going to Southern Seminary. He was encouraging in all of it, and so was Mae. She was right there with me all the time. When I would bring up a problem I could think of, she would help me think through it to say, "It's possible. I think we can do this."

I also learned from Milas that one of the first things necessary would be a recommendation from my church to Southern Seminary. It so happened that our pastor at that time, Lewis McKinney, who took Rev. Boone's place, had studied at Southern Seminary. I went to him with the question about a church recommendation. He said, "We will have to have a deacon's meeting for them to question you before we can write that letter of recommendation, however, I don't see that there will be any problem."

Rev. McKinney had a Called Deacons meeting. He said to me that he thought that instead of just a letter of recommendation, it would be better to license me into the ministry. He felt this would be a stronger kind of recommendation from the church. The deacons questioned me on my sincerity of doing this. They all knew me from the time I was knee-high to a duck, but they were more concerned about my desire to really serve the Lord in this way than anything else. So they recommended to the church, that on a certain day, they would have a licensing service, as part of another service of course, to license me into full-time Christian work with no stipulations as to what it would be. They were leaving that to the Lord and me. All this took place very shortly after that meeting with the deacons.

The licensing was all we needed to verify the fact that I was serious about going ahead with plans to become a minister of music. Mae and I decided to make a trip to Louisville to work out some of the details about a place to live and to get answers to questions I had about the seminary itself, about the diploma and sacred music, etc. Also, we were going to try to find work for Mae. This was all during the summer of 1953. In fact, I remember that it was in August, and if I enrolled as a student at the seminary to begin my study in September, I didn't have much time to make things happen. It's amazing how the Lord opened the way for me though. Mama agreed to keep the children while we made the trip.

I was driving a 1948 Chevrolet Club Coupe at that time. It was just a few days after the church officially licensed me. In those days, we did a lot more driving at night in the summertime for coolness. We didn't have air conditioning in cars back then, at least not in ours. From Rock Hill to Louisville, Kentucky was 850 miles. We drove all night to get there. We only stopped once on the way. I was the only one that could drive; Mae had not learned to drive yet and did not have a driver's license. All the driving was left up to me and I became very tired, to the point that it was becoming dangerous. I remember us pulling off the road into a church yard or some kind of safe place, and we just laid our heads back and snoozed a while. We didn't know what an interstate highway was in those days; there was no such thing. We had four chains of mountains to cross to get from Rock Hill to Louisville. Each of the mountain chains had very crooked roads of course, and you couldn't make good time. It usually took us, on our trips to and from Louisville, 13 hours of traveling to make the trip.

The first thing we did when we got to Louisville was to try to find the seminary. Believe it or not, when I was talking to someone about becoming a student there, Mae was in the hall at Norton Hall, which is the main administration building along with some classrooms, etc. She was walking down the hall and looked on a bulletin board where students would stick notes if they had something they wanted to sell, or a book they wanted to find, or whatever. The students worked together to help each other out in this way. One of the notes there on that bulletin board was that Clifton Baptist Church had begun looking for a church secretary. The man's name was on the note, and it read "if you're interested, please contact Mr. Pound" and it had his number there. Mae called him and told him the story of why we were there. He arranged a meeting on Sunday morning, during Sunday

School, for the committee to talk to Mae about the job. She had had experience as a secretary. She had worked for the Coca-Cola Bottling Company in Rock Hill and other places, and she also had typing and bookkeeping in high school.

That meeting took place during Sunday School on Sunday morning, and we were to leave there that afternoon in order to get back to Rock Hill in time for me to go to work on Monday morning. I'll never forget Mr. Pound saying, "If we wait to have the church act on this decision, these two young people are going to be leaving here this afternoon with an uncertainty. I think it's important enough to make this happen. She's the one we want, so let's have a called business meeting today to vote on it." At the end of that morning service, they called the church in conference, the committee brought the report to the church body, and they voted to hire her as church secretary. All that happened on that particular weekend. If that wasn't the work of the Lord, I don't know what it was!

We also drove out to Seminary Village to see the apartment buildings that were mentioned in the *Baptist Courier* that Mae had already read. Before the Baptists bought the village, it was called Greentree Manor, and they were changing the name of it to Seminary Village. It was a very nice place. Instead of one or two large apartment buildings, they had a building for nearly every letter of the alphabet. Each building had about a half dozen apartments in it. We were not sure about getting a place there to live because it was so recently purchased by the Baptists. There were many people living there who had to move out, and they had to have time to do so. They weren't going to put anybody out on the street. That's a part of the story that will come a little later, as to how we ended up in Apartment G-4, a first floor apartment, which suited us really well.

We left Louisville, going back to Rock Hill, with Mae having a job when we returned. As it happened, they wanted her to come on as soon as she could because they needed a secretary in that position before they started a new church year. We worked it out for her to go back to Louisville a couple of weeks before I was able to move us there. Again, my dear mother took care of the children while I was working and while Mae was in Louisville.

Another beautiful part of the Lord's working in our lives is the fact that Mae was talking with Mrs. Pound about places she might be able to stay for the two weeks while I was trying to wrap things up in Rock Hill and get us moved to Louisville. Mrs. Pound said, "We have plenty of room here. We would love to have you." They were both very lovely people. Mr. Pound worked at one of the banks in Louisville, and Mrs. Pound did not work outside the home. This arrangement worked out really well because Mae was working on the Louisville end of things, to find us a place to live, and other things that needed to be arranged while I was working all I could at the Aragon Mill for us to have some money. She talked to the man who was in charge of the apartments and told him what we needed. She wanted to know if there was any way we could get an apartment there, in order to move before school started in September. He said, "We do not have one available at all, and don't know when we will have one." I began sweating it out, thinking "I'm going to have to get this furniture to Louisville, and we need to move on this for me to go to school this year." I did not want to be there a whole semester at school without our furniture.

Mr. Pound comes in to the story again because he knew the man that was in charge of Seminary Village. It was the Superintendent of Building & Grounds for the seminary, which included Seminary Village. His name was T. R. Allen. Mr. Allen told Mr. Pound to get in touch with me and tell me to bring my furniture on, and "we'll make it happen somehow by the time he gets here." Over a week had passed without any certainty about a place to live. I was still working at the Aragon Mill as long as I could before packing up furniture and leaving. As soon as Mae got word from Mr. Pound about what Mr. Allen had said, she called me. They got me to the phone in the mill, and she told me what Mr. Allen had said. I said, "Do you mean he doesn't have a place?" She said, "He said to come on; we'll work it out somehow."

I left the mill immediately because the job I had made it possible. I drove to Charlotte that afternoon to see about renting a trailer to haul our furniture. I needed a large trailer, even though we were not able to take everything. The apartment was not all that large, but the house we were living in was not so large, therefore, we were able to get the necessities. We didn't have U-Haul back then; it was Yellow Trailer. When I got to Charlotte, to the trailer place, they said, "We're sorry. We don't have one as large as you need. We have trailers 14 feet long and 8 feet wide, but we don't have one on the lot right now." I said, "What is the nearest place where I can go find one?" He said, "We may have one in Greensboro." I said, "Call them and ask them." He did, and I was on my way very shortly after that, going all the way to Greensboro to get us a trailer. I had put a trailer hitch on the back of that Chevrolet earlier, and everything was working out for me to go get what I needed. It was an open trailer, with no top or enclosure like they have today. It was more like a two-horse wagon. In fact, it had a fifth wheel. The whole front axle turned to go around a curve, not just the wheels turning. Traveling that far with our furniture, we had to have a way of waterproofing in case it rained, of course. Well, Dad talked to Mr. Moss, who was in charge of shipping and all the loading and unloading of bales of cotton and so forth there at the mill, and they let us have a tarpaulin, large enough to cover that whole trailer, 14 feet long and 8 feet wide, and coming down the sides as far as it needed to come to waterproof our furniture. Earl, Dean, and Daddy helped me load our furniture on the trailer the next day. Earl said, "You mean to tell me you're going to load this furniture and go toward Louisville without knowing for sure that you have a place to stay?" I said, "Mr. Allen said to come on, and we're on our way! The Lord's going to work this out because he wants me to go there."

We loaded the furniture on a Saturday (I don't remember the date). We were not able to leave Rock Hill until Sunday night. Dad had responsibilities in his church, leading the music, and we weren't able to leave until after the service on Sunday night. When we got all that furniture loaded on that trailer, it was very heavy. All the while, I wondered if my little Club Coupe was going to be able to pull this trailer. When

I pulled it from Greensboro to Rock Hill, it was empty, so I knew it was going to be a big load for my car. Quite frankly, I was not afraid of it not pulling the trailer, I was more afraid of *stopping* the trailer. The trailer did not have brakes on it like travel trailers have today—they're hooked up in such a way that when you brake the towing vehicle, it also brakes the trailer. We didn't have such back then. At that time, Daddy owned a 1947 Buick Roadmaster, the biggest and heaviest Buick they made in those days.

So the trip began on Sunday night after church, and by the time we actually got away with the two vehicles, it was ten or eleven o'clock. David, Donna, Mama and I were in my car, and Daddy, of course, was in his car, and towing the trailer. (We didn't have Judi at that time; she was not in the world until several years later.) Mae and I had taken trips with the little Club Coupe that we had, and I was able to put apple crates on either side of the drive shaft with a board or two across it. This made a nice area for the two children, who were small at that time, to ride, play, sleep, or do whatever they wanted to do except fight. Of course, Donna was not old enough to fight. She was still in diapers. Mae had been in the process of training Donna and just about had her where she could potty on her own. She was about 18 months old. However, Mae told Mama that if it would be easier on her to not continue training Donna, it would be okay. It was a lot easier for us to change diapers than to try to train her; we were so busy doing other things.

We pulled out of Rock Hill about eleven o'clock that Sunday night, and Daddy was only driving about 25 miles per hour. I thought he was driving slowly until we got out of town, then he would step it on up to 50 or 55, but he didn't. He kept on driving at a slow speed. I said to Mama, "If he's not going to drive any faster than that, we'll be a couple of days getting to Louisville" because I had already driven it a couple of times without the trailer, and it was a very long trip—at least 13 hours.

Dad made a wrong turn, realized it was wrong, then stopped. I stopped too, and walked up to where he was. We discussed how to correct the situation without trying to back that trailer up. It was almost impossible to back that kind of trailer. While I was talking to him, I said, "Dad, you're going to have to drive a little faster, or we're going to be a long, long time getting to Louisville." Dad made another wrong turn later, which slowed us down a little bit, but not much. After all, he was going all out to try to help me get to Louisville, and I didn't dare fuss at him. We had no problems at all except the tarpaulin had a tendency to work its way loose when it was catching the wind. Dad said, "I'll put the qui-ee-tous on that!" (That was a word he used when he said he was going to fix something that was hard to fix.) We stopped in a little town and went into a hardware store. He got some roofing nails with big heads on them. The trailer was wood, and he borrowed a hammer and nailed that tarp to the trailer. We didn't have any more trouble with that.

The only other problem we had was when we were going up a really steep mountain. To make things difficult, the road was under construction. By this time, I was driving the Buick, and Dad was driving my car. In order for me to get around that construction equipment, I had to drive around loose gravel where they were getting ready to do some paving. This made the back wheels on the Buick to spin, and I couldn't get any traction. I was kind of digging two holes in the gravel and not going anywhere. One of the very big trucks being used in the construction came up behind the trailer and very easily bumped that trailer and pushed me up that gravel road until I got past the construction. I sure did appreciate it, too. I didn't know what in the world I was going to do if we got stuck there and couldn't get out.

After I started driving the Buick, we made a lot better time. I guess it was because I was young and foolish and more of a daredevil. I moved quite a bit faster than Daddy was going, however I didn't do anything real dangerous. The top speed limit in those days was 55, but driving through those mountains, we couldn't drive that fast anyway. I was still driving when we got to Lexington, driving through town on Highway 60. Down in the business section of town, we came to an intersection. A car was in front of me, and evidently the driver thought he was about to make a wrong turn, and he stopped suddenly. There I was with that heavy load of furniture behind the Buick, and I locked all four wheels to get stopped. I had to turn a little bit, which caused the trailer to jack-knife, to the point that it rocked. It never did turn over, but it rocked like it was going to. Dad and Mama said they thought any second they would see my furniture scattered all over that road. It didn't happen.

Louisville was about 60 or 70 miles away, so we were making good time. Not too far outside of Lexington, toward Louisville, we stopped for a little rest stop. Dad said, "Son, I've gone just about as far as I can go without some rest." Of course, I said, "Well, we'll rest a while," and we did. I was a whole lot younger and anxious to get there, but we stopped for a rest for him. I was tired too but not as tired as he was. I was also anxious to get there because I had a good-looking brunette waiting on me, and her name was Mae!

We got to Louisville to the Pounds' house, late afternoon or early evening. One thing that helped us on time was that we had entered Central Time Zone, which meant we had gained an hour. I drove that Buick with the furniture around to the Pounds' home. Mae was looking for us. We didn't have cell phones to call ahead. We didn't want to stop to go to a telephone booth, but she was anxious too for us to get there. She knew what a long trip it would be. We got to the Pounds' house, and Mae came out to meet us. I was never so glad to see anybody as I was to see her that day. I had not seen her in two weeks. One of the first things I said to her, of course, was "Do we have a place to live?" She said, "Yes, we do." I was thanking the Lord. She said, "We're going to Apartment G-4." That was Building G, and Apartment #4.

While we were traveling from the Pounds' home to our new home, I was wondering how in the world Daddy and I were going to be able to unload all that furniture. It was already getting late in the day, and darkness was soon to come. That always slows us down on something like that, you know. We pulled up in front of the building. Thank goodness, as I looked, we didn't have any steps to go up, except one step to go into the hallway, and our apartment was immediately to the left. As it turned out, we didn't have to get any help to unload the furniture because just as soon as we uncovered our things, students came from several different directions to unload the trailer. That's seminary for you! Of course, we pitched in and did what we could, but they were on top of it and had the trailer unloaded before we knew what we were doing. I'm just thankful there were already a few students living out there because they were the ones who came to help us. A theology student, Gaskin, and his family lived right across the hall from our apartment. His wife was kind enough to offer to add enough to their meal to feed us supper since we were going to be working to get that furniture unloaded. Gestures like that made us feel really good because we knew we were among friends already, and we were going to be where we could get help if we needed it. To tell you the truth, Mae and I didn't know what it was like to be away from home. We married so young, and this was actually the first time we had moved away from home. After all, our home was already there.

I remember one time earlier, when the mill where I worked was curtailing (meaning they were not running full-time). The days I didn't work I didn't get paid, and we were hurting for money. Jerry Buchanan had heard that MacDonell Aircraft Corporation in St. Louis, Missouri was hiring a lot of people and paying good money. He and I got in our '41 Chevrolet and went all the way out there, stayed a few days, and we decided we were better off at home because the cost of living was so much there, we'd be in the hole to start with. After all, Mae's father ran a grocery store, and I knew we wouldn't go hungry. I think the Lord was already working on me to do what we had just done in getting me to Louisville to seminary. He had greater things for me to do.

The next day, we dropped the trailer off in Louisville. Mama and Dad left almost immediately for Rock Hill. We had just a few days to get settled in our new apartment before I had to go matriculate for my studies at the seminary.

The seminary was on one side of Lexington Avenue going into Louisville, one of the main streets. Across Lexington was a mansion that was given to the seminary by B. B. Cook, who was a Southern Baptist who raised cattle. He had moved to a ranch in the edge of town, and he had several car dealerships there in Louisville. That mansion he had given to Southern Baptists became Cook Hall, named after him of course. Cook Hall was where the music school was. There were some classes over on the main campus, but most of our music classes were in that old mansion.

I went over to Cook Hall to talk to Doris Jean Bowman, who headed up the office there in Cook Hall. I learned from her that there was some scholarship money available, but I had to try out for it. She said, "You'll need to prepare a couple of songs and get an accompanist. It's going to happen here at Cook Hall." Dr. Walter Dahlin, who directed the Seminary Chorus, and Farrold Stephens, who was a voice teacher, would be in the room to hear us sing or play or whatever a student could do. I said, "I'll give it a try. I don't have anything much to lose." So I pulled out *Comfort Ye My People* again, that Milas MacDonnell heard me sing, and he twisted my arm and sent me to the seminary. I went in with an accompanist and met Dr. Dahlin and Mr. Stevens for the first time. After we talked for a minute to get acquainted, they asked what I was going to sing. I said, "Well, I'm going to sing *Comfort Ye My People* from Handel's *Messiah*." Farrold Stephens said, "Are you going to do *Every Valley*?" I immediately thought about the times when I was a kid, trying to learn to sing *Every Valley* there at 84 Frasier Street. I said, "No, I'm not prepared to sing *Every Valley*, but I would like to sing *Comfort Ye*." They said, "That's fine. Go right ahead." I sang the piece. Farrold Stephens spoke up and said, "How much voice training have you had?" I said "I have never had voice lessons." I'll never forget what he said. He said, "That's the best. You're a natural." That made me feel better immediately. He knew that with the proper help, I could become a pretty good vocalist by being a natural. By the way, I got the scholarship, which amounted to about $125. That doesn't seem like much money now, but it sure was back then, especially after we had had all kinds of expenses getting to Louisville.

I was not fortunate enough to have voice lessons with Farrold Stephens. They assigned me to Audrey Nossaman, who was good for me as a start, but I did not really blossom, so to speak, until the next year, when I went with Farrold Stephens. I was able to make that change without hurting anybody's feelings because Audrey Nossaman left to go to New York to teach there and to sing opera.

I studied two and a half years in music at Southern Seminary. At last, I was doing what I felt called to do in life. It started out as a three-year study to get a diploma in sacred music, which would equip me to go to a small church somewhere and be their minister of music. I also had to study a certain amount of religious education because so many of the churches were calling men to do both music and education. However, Dr. Forrest Heeren decided that a diploma student should not be required to take some of the courses the graduate students were taking. I studied in the same classes with graduate students, but some of the courses, like 16th Century Counterpoint, he felt should be taken out of our curriculum. That made me happy because I didn't feel like I needed that anyway, and it meant that I would be getting through the school one semester earlier, which I did. So I began in September 1953, and studied two and a half years. I graduated in January 1956. I wouldn't take anything for having gone to that school and prepared for what I've done for 55 years.

Part of my training at the seminary required that I do a substantial recital before I could graduate, which I did. Dr. Heeren also said he thought that a diploma student should not be expected to give the same recital in difficulty and length that the graduate students were giving, but Farrold Stephens was my teacher, and he said, "I wouldn't think of having you cut back on that. You're going to do a full recital." I sang five different languages. Farrold Stephens meant a lot to me in all of this. He was a very fine singer himself, and he knew how to put it across to me so that I understood what I needed to do.

He meant a lot to me in other ways too. When it came time for me to have a class in vocal literature, he was the teacher. When it was time for me to have vocal pedagogy, which is the study of how to teach voice, he was the teacher. When it was time for me to take Italian diction, he was the teacher.

These subjects were shared by all the faculty at different times. I'll always believe God put him in that slot for me because in everything related to voice those last two years I studied, he was the teacher. Mae has said a number of times that I was like a sponge when I went to the seminary. I soaked up so much of the training in such a short time. Remember, not bragging; just facts. I finished my seminary training toward a diploma and received it in January of 1956.

Charles rode his bicycle often as a teenager.

Charles and Mae began their courtship in high school.

Charles and Mae during high school

Charles sang for numerous weddings and funerals as a teenager.

Charles rode his whizzer motor bike to Ebenezer to visit Mae.

David Wayne Crocker was born
November 1, 1949

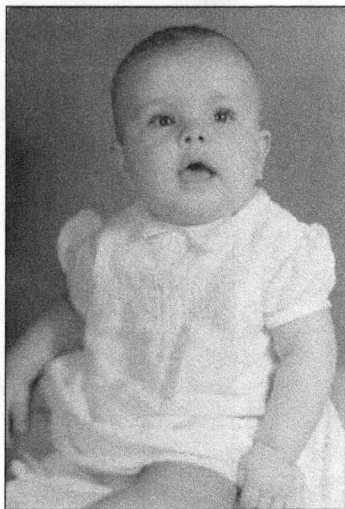

Donna Ruth Crocker was born
January 3, 1952

Norton Hall at The Southern Baptist
Theological Seminary, 1954

Seminary graduate, January 1956

Seminary Choir; Charles is fourth from the left, back row.

9

First Churches

My first church out of the seminary was First Baptist Church in Kershaw, South Carolina. Kershaw is about 45 or 50 miles below Rock Hill. I went to Kershaw on New Year's weekend. New Year's Day was on Sunday, and I was scheduled to go back to Louisville the next day. Mae stayed in Louisville, and I had David and Donna with me. I was giving a ride to another seminary student, named Ted Robinson, who happened to live next door to Dad. I drove with just the two children to Rock Hill and spent the weekend at Mama and Daddy's. They had already moved out of their new house back to the village, down on Long Street, just a house or two from where we lived when I had pneumonia. I participated in the morning service at Kershaw and sang a solo. I remember it being *I See His Blood upon the Rose* by Hagemon. That was one of the songs I had just sung in my recital, and I had it memorized. I talked to the committee that afternoon, and they said they would like very much to have me come and work in their church. As I think back, I'm sure that having a church that close to Rock Hill influenced my thinking more than I realized at the time. It was the only natural thing to do, to be close to Mom and Dad. Dean and Earl were in Rock Hill at the time. To be able to go back to that area was very appealing to me. That did not affect my working for the church in any way that I could tell.

On the way back to Louisville, I was giving Ted Robinson a ride back to the seminary. We met on Monday, which was a holiday. We got in the car. Ted said, "I'll be glad to help you with the driving." I said, "Well, I'll let you do that, but I'll drive the first hundred miles or so, and you can drive the next hundred or so, and we'll just work it that way, and it won't be hard on either one of us." David and Donna were in the back seat of the car. They had a play area back there, and they could play or sleep, or whatever they wanted to do. The car that I owned when we moved to Louisville was a '48 Chevrolet Club Coupe. Now, two and a half years later, it was about to give out on me, and I took advantage of B. B. Cook's offer to help any seminary student who needed a car. He said, "Don't let him leave without a car, if you have to balloon the note as big as the side of the house. Put him in a car." So he did, and I was driving a brand new '55 Chevrolet that we had bought just the year before, in February. So off we went to Louisville.

We got to Asheville. All of this was traveling on the old roads—no super highways—and we went right through the middle of Asheville and on toward Marshall, and down Main Street in Marshall. We drove out the other side of Marshall and had gone up a fair sized mountain and were going down the other side. Ted was taking the curves pretty fast, and I cautioned him two or three times. I said, "Ted, I've driven this road a number of times. Don't let a curve sneak up on you. You need to slow down." He kind of looked at me and grinned, as if to say, "You think I don't know how to drive." I said, "I know you've done a lot of driving, but you're not accustomed to this car, and you need to slow down a little bit." We went on down the mountain, and he hit a curve that was a lot sharper than he thought. He lost control of the car, and it so happened we went into a ditch that was on the mountain side of the road and not a drop-off. I've always been thankful for that. If it had been the opposite, the car would have rolled and there's no telling where it would have stopped. The right front wheel of that brand new car dug into the bank, and it bent the axle and wheel back against the car. It could not be driven at all.

The first thing I did was jump out of the car and check on David and Donna. They were crying because the accident scared them. They did not get hurt in any way, but they were frightened. I'll never forget what David said when I asked, "Are you sure the two of you are okay?" They calmed down and stopped crying. David started crying again and said, "I am sure am glad Mama's not with us!" I said, "I am too now, but why do you say that, David?" He said "'Cause she would have gotten hurt! She is so fluffy!"

There we were between Marshall and Hot Springs, on the side of a mountain. Being the second day of January, it was so cold the ground you could see was spewed up. It had rained, or there was enough moisture in the ground it had spewed up into icicles. We couldn't run the engine in the car to stay warm, and I had to do something to keep the two children warm. I dug their suitcase out of the back of the car, and opened it. They had two heavy coats in there, with a lighter coat they were going to be wearing around the house in the cold weather. I put the lighter coat on them, and a coat that my mother made—one for David and one for Donna—out of a Navy peacoat that Earl wore when he was in the Navy. She couldn't cut the coat down in size because they were very small at the time. David had just started to school, and was part of the way through the first grade. Donna was a preschooler. They had so many clothes on to stay warm that their arms wouldn't hang straight down.

I said, "What are we going to do? We're going to have to have a wrecker to tow this car in. It cannot be driven." Ted said, "I'm sorry this happened. I will go on down to Hot Springs and see if I can't find a wrecker to come back up here to tow us in." I sort of felt like we were closer to Hot Springs than Marshall, but I thought, I will try to go the other way, toward Marshall, but I didn't make that decision until we had waited and waited and waited for Ted to come back with a wrecker. I decided I was going to have to do something quick because the day was passing on, and I sure didn't want to be up there on the side of that mountain after dark with my two children.

Soon after the wreck, a sheriff drove up, and he said, "We're going to have to get this car out of here because too much of it is sticking out on the road." I said, "Sir, if you will do that, I will be glad. The car won't move, and my buddy has gone to try to find a wrecker to tow it in." He left, and right after that, a car with two or three seminary students stopped. They saw what had happened, and they offered to take us on to where we needed to go, especially to Louisville if we needed it. I said, "No, I can't leave because my friend has gone to get help, and I have to get this car somewhere to have it fixed." So they went on, and I decided, "Children, we're going back to Marshall and find somebody to tow this car in." They said, "Okay, Daddy. That's what we'll do." We walked across the road in that sharp curve, and walked up the road just a little ways to get off that curve. The first car that came by was a man and his wife going toward Marshall, and I don't remember if I thumbed or just waved my hand. They saw the car was in trouble, and they pulled over. I said, "Can you please help me?" They said, "Is that your car?" I said, "Yes it is" and I quickly told them what had happened. They said, "By all means, get in, and we will go down to Marshall to get you some help."

We did that. I locked the trunk of the car with our belongings in it, and got in the car with David and Donna and the man and his wife. They took us in to Marshall, and everything was closed up, being a holiday. I was able to get in touch with someone who had a wrecker, and they agreed to go up and tow my car in. I had to leave the car with them. They were the Ford dealer in Marshall. They agreed to fix the car.

I put in a call to Mama because Daddy was working in the mill at that time. I told her what had happened, and I hastened to say that nobody was hurt, but the car was messed up to the point that I could not drive it. "I'm having it towed in. Do you think you could get Daddy in touch with me? (I gave her the phone number) I need Daddy to come get us." Instead of it being just Daddy, it was Dean and Daddy in

Dean's car. They came up there. It was getting close to dark by that time. We had already been in a restaurant there, the Rock Café. They're still in business down in Marshall. After I talked to Mama on the phone, I said, "Children, let's go to the Rock Café over here and get us some supper." So we did. I felt so sorry for the children. I said, "Now, I want you to eat whatever you want. We've got to get some food in you." They had not had a bite to eat since that morning at Mama and Daddy's. I had a menu in my hand (they couldn't read by then). I said, "Donna, what would you like?" She said, "I wan' cheese sammich." I said, "Oh no, Donna, let's get you a good hot meal, a meat and two or three vegetables, something real good and warm. We've been in the cold all day, and I'd feel better about it if you'd get a good plate lunch." She said, "Daddy, I wan' a cheese sammich." She said it so pitifully and began to tear up a little. I said, "If you want a cheese sandwich, and that's what you really want, you've got it!" I ordered it. I don't remember what David ordered; I just remember laughing about the fact that she wanted a cheese sandwich when she could have anything she wanted.

Daddy and Dean came, and we got in the car, and felt safe and warm, and all the other good things. We had had a good meal. We went back to Rock Hill. We left the next morning in Daddy's '51 Buick Special. Dad lived about two good mill village blocks from the mill where he was still working. He was able to work it out with someone to come by and pick him up to get him to church. We didn't think about renting a car and didn't have the money to do that. I'm not even sure they had rental cars in those days.

We left Rock Hill, the two children, Ted Robinson, and I, hoping to get all the way to Louisville. I did not even mention it, nor did Ted mention it to me about driving. I drove that car every inch of the way back to Louisville. Actually, I'm glad Daddy was able to let us have his car because we needed a car more than Daddy did, to get Mae to Clifton Baptist Church as church secretary, and get the children to child care, and I had to get to seminary to class. A lot of those classes were at eight o'clock in the morning.

There's an interesting story pertaining to the first few weeks I was on the job in Kershaw. To tell this story, I have to digress to the seminary days, when I had strep throat. I was running a fever of 104 degrees. The doctor I saw to begin with said he could not see anything about my throat that would cause that kind of a fever and make me so sick. I'm glad I went to another doctor there on Frankfurt Avenue. He said he could understand why I was running such a fever and was so ill, because I had strep throat. He was afraid that it had gone so long that it was going to turn into meningitis or rheumatic fever or scarlet fever, those diseases that stem from a strep germ. He said, "Anytime you get a sore throat like that, you get attention right away!"

Now, back to Kershaw. About the second week we were there, I came down with a sore throat. I didn't think it was strep, but it was sore enough that I felt like I needed to get some help. I did not know any of the doctors, so I went to the church secretary and explained my problem. I asked her if she knew where I could find a doctor, or if she would recommend one. She said, "There's a doctor set up in an old house, about a block down the street." She gave me the phone number and the name of the doctor, whom I called immediately. I explained my problem and they said, "Come on in. We'll take a look at you."

Fortunately, it was close, so I just walked down to the doctor's office. I went in the door, and immediately the receptionist took me back to a room in the back of the house. When we entered the room, she said, "Go ahead and take off all your clothes, shoes and all, and put this gown on" which she handed me. I questioned it, saying, "All of my clothes?" She said, "Yes, you need to take off all your clothes and put that gown on." I thought that was awfully strange, but I also thought, well, this is a doctor with a new patient. He's going to give me a complete physical maybe, to set up some medical records for the future. So, I began taking my clothes off. I removed my shirt and started down with my pants. About that time, the doctor came in the room, and he said, "You are the one who came in to be circumcised, aren't you?" I immediately yanked my pants back up and I said, "No, doctor! You've got the wrong one! I'm here for a sore throat!" He apologized, of course.

When I was treated for the sore throat and leaving the office, the ladies who were there in the office had a big laugh when I went by. It was embarrassing not only for me but for the doctor who would assume I was there for that, instead of something else. It so happened there was a man due in the office any time that was to have a circumcision. The doctor and the nurses thought I was the one. He didn't say "I'm glad I caught that" before he had a chance to come at me with a knife or a pair of scissors.

Kershaw was a very small town of about 2,000 people. It was a textile community, and it was small enough for that story to get around town in what seemed to me like just a day or so. I would be walking down the street and people would yell at me across the street, "How's your throat doing?" I knew what they meant, and they would laugh when they said it.

Due to a misunderstanding I had with the Kershaw church and pastor, I was only there six months. They wanted a person who could do music and education, and I did not know that until I went to the church. I knew I was not as qualified as they wanted me to be in religious education. I thought it would be better if they had somebody who was qualified. As soon as I began my work there, I was already feeling that I needed more training, especially in the basic college studies, such as English, Math, History, and those things are the basis for all education.

I tried to pray earnestly for the Lord's leadership once again, and it came. Ordinarily, when it would be known that a person had only been in a church for six months, they would not get an invitation to move to another church, but I did. That's when we moved from Kershaw to Greenville, South Carolina. I became minister of music at Leawood Baptist Church, with Dr. B. F. Rogers as pastor. Before we moved to Greenville, I talked to the proper people at Furman University in Greenville, and worked it out so I could do some study and be the minister of music at the church too. Leawood Baptist

Church was good for me; the people there were very cordial and very patient with me. We made many very dear friends, some of whom have passed away, but there are others who remember us, and we talk to them on occasion. We see them fairly often and enjoy their friendship.

In this case, the church was like a sponge, soaking up everything I had to offer; therefore, I was able to do some very interesting things in music. One of the big things I did was to lead them through a very elaborate Easter program, which called for sets, some costuming, etc. The choir loft looked like a green hill—it was covered with artificial grass from the funeral home—with dogwood blossoms all over it, and a cross at the top of it. We also had an open tomb made out of papier mache' that was opened toward the end of that service to represent the resurrection of our Lord. The interesting thing about this is that all of the scenery was put into place on a Sunday afternoon. No one in the group helping with it even thought that we would not get it done, so we made it happen. The choir sang behind that hill, and we had photo slides being shown on the front side of that hill, with related songs and scripture being presented from behind the hill. At a certain time, when we got to the resurrection, all the lights were out, and we had a wire fastened to the door of the tomb to open it, and bright lights shined inside. This made for a big production for that church. Remember—no brag; just facts.

We were at Leawood for about three years and enjoyed all kinds of fellowship with church members, such as going to Santee Cooper with some of the guys on fishing trips. The church bought two old school buses that had been discarded and made one good one out of them. I used that bus to take the youth choir on trips. I enjoyed taking them to Rock Hill and having them sing at the church where my dad was part-time minister of music. (About the time I left for the seminary, Dad had decided to take on working in a paid position for a church or two. He continued working at the Aragon Mill, but he did the church music on Wednesday nights and on Sundays. He was at Calvary Baptist Church, adjacent to the industrial mill village, at this time.)

My time at Leawood Baptist Church was a good start for me in music ministry. I was able to use what I had learned at seminary to help the choirs produce better choral sounds and to help lead the church in worship. I was getting training of a different kind, as a church staff member and learning more about how to lead, which would be especially important as I continued in ministry in the following years.

Leawood Baptist Church choirs. Donna is first on the left, front row. David is on the third row, fifth from the left.

10

Griffin and Nashville

After about three years at Leawood, First Baptist Church in Griffin, Georgia called me to become their minister of music. It was a much larger church with a lot more opportunities to stretch my abilities as minister of music. It caused me to grow more in this field, which is what I needed. All the while, I still had the desire to finish my basic education.

During the time we were in Griffin, I was able to do a good bit of game hunting. The minister of education, Tom Dean, was also a student at Southern Seminary when I was there, however, he was in Religious Education and I was in Music, but we knew each other because we were both originally from South Carolina. He was an avid hunter, even more so than I was. We became interested in deer hunting. By that time, a good many deer had moved into parts of Georgia and there was open season on deer. The limit was only one deer per season at the time I was there, and that had to be a buck, not a doe.

There was a family in our church in Griffin that owned a large tract of land just east of Monticello. (This happens to be the town where my brother Dean pastored a church for about 15 years.) This family had about 1000 acres that was bordered by Murder Creek. We would go every year and do some scouting before the deer season, which began the first part of November. So, in 1964, once again we went to that area to scout for deer sign so we would know where to still-hunt. We did still-hunting, meaning you find a place to sit down or camouflage and be still and wait on the deer to come by. I found a place where there were some really recent deer signs (droppings). A buck will rub his antlers on a tree when it's rutting season, and things like that would tell me that deer had been using that area. There was a tree that had obviously been broken over when it was a small tree, but it didn't die. It grew on up to be a full grown tree. Where it had broken it had healed, and it looked like a large limb that went in a slope from the tree down to the ground. It was heavy enough that I could step on it and walk right on up to the trunk of the tree, and I had a good place to sit down.

In fact, I did something that made it an even better deer stand, something that I was later teased about. I went to the bicycle shop and got an old seat with the seat post. The seat post is what attaches the seat to the bicycle. It's a shaft about three-quarters of an inch in diameter. I took a ¾-inch wood bit, and the tool you use it with, called a brace, went over there, walked up that tree, and right next to the main trunk of the tree, I bored a hole deep enough to put that seat post down in it. I had one of the best deer stands in the country! It would swivel around and I could move almost 360 degrees except the main trunk would keep me from seeing part of the area. But that was okay. I had plenty of land to look at. I went over the first day of the season, November 1, 1964, and had my 30:06 Winchester ready to get my first, and maybe my only deer of the season. It was still dark; we always went into the woods before daylight so we could get to our stand without spooking a deer. About an hour after good daylight, I heard footsteps like a deer coming through the woods. I didn't see him until he came out into a slightly open area and stopped. The deer was about 50 yards or so from where I was. I took my Winchester and dropped him. It was a 10-pointer, meaning the points on the antlers are counted in that way. Usually the bigger the deer, the bigger the antlers, and you're after a trophy as well as good eating. The only bad thing about it was my season, as far as carrying a gun and killing a deer was concerned, was over. However, there was nothing to keep me from going into the woods and enjoying the outdoors and the beautiful nature that God has given us.

So, I thought about David, who was 14 years old at the time. He had done some hunting with me, for other kinds of game, but he had not hunted any deer with a gun. I asked him if he wanted to go over with me and let me help him get a deer. He said he sure would.

I guess it was on a Saturday because he wasn't in school. We made plans to go hunting together. We set a date—it was exactly one week later from the day the season started. Years before this, I had taken a British 303 Enfield rifle, which was the British war weapon, and I had converted it into a sportsman rifle for hunting. I put it on a different kind of stock and polished it all up. It was a really nice piece. We got up early, stopped in Jackson where hunters gathered in a restaurant for breakfast, ate us a really good breakfast, and left there in time to get to Murder Creek and into the woods where the stand was. There was an old logging road that I could drive down quite a ways, but I didn't want to drive the car all the way to the stand area. So, we stopped early and got out. David got the rifle, and I told him, "Let me tell you something, now. You be real careful." I talked about how I had learned gun safety when I was in Boy Scouts. I said, "But, I wanted to tell you, that if you kill a deer today, that's your rifle. It would be my gift to you for you to enjoy in years to come."

As we were walking toward the stand, we stopped along the way for a little bit and just listened. In the woods ahead of us we heard several deer kind of running along. They make a very distinctive sound when they're hopping through the woods, you know. There were at least two or three of them by the way it sounded. I said, "David, I think that probably was several doe." We couldn't kill a doe in those days, in that part of the country. So we walked on, a little ways beyond, probably 30 or 40 yards beyond where we saw tracks where those deer had run through the woods. I said to David, "Let's step off over here in the bushes, off this deer trail and be real quiet because those were doe, and I'll bet you a buck will be coming through here on the same trail pretty soon." I said that because it was the rutting season. Rutting season is when they mate and the doe gets pregnant and they raise young ones.

So we moved off that trail for just a little ways. It was just like we had ordered it from Sears & Roebuck—I heard one deer coming, and David did too. The woods were dry enough that you could hear each of the four hooves hitting the dry leaves, even though it was packed down some with the deer coming through. We couldn't see the deer yet. The woods were thick enough, and there was enough undergrowth that we could not see the deer, but we could hear it. Well, he kept on walking—he was coming right toward us. He made a little bit of a turn, but he was still on the trail beside us. I said, "David, don't shoot until I tell you to. I mean it! *Don't shoot 'til I tell you to!*" David was trembling and I was excited. I cannot tell you how excited I was because I was fairly certain we were going to get him a deer. That deer walked right out into the open and stopped, and he wasn't more than 15 or 20 yards from us, broadsided, and he was looking right toward us. A deer has a very keen sense of smell, and I think he smelled us and that's why he stopped. That's one of the reasons you have a deer stand in a tree if you can because the scent from your body will tend to rise from body heat and the deer won't smell you. The deer was standing there, and David had his rifle up to his shoulder. I said, "Don't shoot....don't shoot..." and about that time the deer walked out into the open, and before I could say "don't shoot" again, David pulled the trigger. WHAM! The deer broke and ran like you've never seen one run before. I didn't see how on earth he could have missed that deer. He could have almost taken his gun and reached out and hit him on the head. I said, "David Crocker, if you missed that deer, I'm gonna shoot *you!*" Well, the deer ran like they will do very often even when they're hurt. They will run for a ways and then you have to find them. We walked in the direction that the deer ran, and David was looking in one direction while I looked in another. I said, "Boy, I hope we got that deer!" About that time, we both saw his white tail. The deer was lying on the ground with his rear end toward us. That white bob tail jumped out at us. The deer was dead. David killed him, and his Daddy was happy. David said, "Daddy, I'm gonna yell! I'm gonna yell!" I said, "Man, turn loose and yell! I'm happy too!" I wouldn't take anything for having been with my son when he killed a deer. That's something that doesn't happen very often, even with the most experienced hunters.

Andrew Blake had his truck not too far from there. He was one of our hunting buddies and a member of our church. He drove his truck down as far as he could, and we cut a pole and carried the deer to his truck. We loaded up and headed toward Griffin, both of us just grinning like mules eating briars! The only thing I didn't like about that episode was that David's deer was bigger than the one that I killed the week before. He wasn't supposed to do that! I took him over there to kill a deer, but he wasn't supposed to kill one bigger than mine. I've never let him forget it. You can come to our house at 12 Chunn's View Drive in Asheville, and see both of those deer heads mounted on a plaque in our den. David never fails to count the points on his and then count the ones on mine. His was eleven points, and mine was only ten. Doggone it, his deer was bigger than mine and weighed more than mine too!

But the story doesn't end there. It was in Griffin that I began my interest in the child's voice. Much of it was due to my working with Fletcher Wolfe and the Atlanta Boy Choir, doing solo work, during which time I was analyzing the sounds of the boys and taking it back to Griffin. I had my children produce those same kinds of sounds, insofar as possible. I challenged the children in my church to make beautiful sounds in singing, and I also challenged them in doing choral literature.

When they sang for the district festival which was held in Atlanta, they were graded down because of a misunderstanding we had about the festival rules. The judges were apologizing to me for having to do that, because it was an unusually good sounding group of boys and girls. In order to correct that mistake before we went to the state festival, we had to work up a new piece, which we did in one rehearsal. We took one of the pieces we did in Atlanta to the state festival. They did a very difficult piece by George Frederic Handel, which was a children's chorus from his oratorio *Judas Maccabeus*. It was entitled *O Lovely Peace*. We received not only a Superior rating, which included a lot of beautiful remarks by the judges, we also were asked to sing when the whole festival gathered. The festival was split up into different areas where different choirs were singing in different places there at the assembly grounds because it was such a large festival. We were asked to sing for the entire festival, which had never been done before, and maybe not since. They sang the Handel number.

I didn't realize that while all this was taking place, Dr. William Reynolds, who was in the music department at the Sunday School Board in Nashville, Tennessee, was listening to us and having great thoughts about making an invitation to us. I did not know it at the time, but they were looking for a choir to record the first and only junior choir Christmas cantata, written by Robert Graham. They were trying to find a group to record it to be used as a demonstration recording for other boys and girls to learn the music. The title of the cantata was *Lo! A Star!*

When Bill Reynolds went back to Nashville and told them he believed he had found the choir to do that recording, Paul Green, who was in charge of all recording for the music department, wrote me a letter and asked for an audition tape. He did not tell me why he wanted it, and I had no idea this was about to happen. This was before we sang at the festival. This is where my interest in recording paid off. I was able to set up recording equipment there with my Sony tape recorder and tape the boys and girls, very much like a recording session. When Paul Green heard the tape, he immediately called me and wanted to know if I would agree to record the cantata.

We accepted the invitation to do the recording, and my church in Griffin contracted with a professional recording company in Atlanta to bring equipment to Griffin and record that cantata. That recording was heard all over the United States, and people automatically put me in a slot as being a children's choir specialist. This was no desire of my own; this is the way it happened. From then on and until I retired, I was asked to be guest conductor at state festivals all over the southeast and some northern states. Remember—no brag; just fact.

There was one chorus in that cantata we recorded that was called *Clip Clop*. It was the donkey that would be carrying Mary, walking along "clip-clop, clip-clop." This is what the girls and boys were singing while some solo work was happening above it. I became known as "Ol' Clip-Clop." Interestingly enough, I was not paid anything for doing that recording, and the boys and girls only received a copy of the cantata on recording. This was okay for me because I wasn't in it for the money anyway. The fact that this was the very first one of these recordings, there was no procedure already in process. The next year, we had about 60 children to enroll in the choir, and we had to find a larger room for rehearsals.

After that recording was made, we were also asked to do others. We did *Lord Most Holy* by Rosemary Cooper and two recordings of children's hymns from the new *Junior Choir Hymnal*, which were done in the recording session with the Atlanta Symphony String Quartet. Also, my older children's choir was invited to go to Kansas City, Missouri, and sing for the Church Music Conference of the Southern Baptist Convention.

While we lived in Griffin, David and Donna went through elementary and some of junior high school. One interesting little story about Donna at a young age is the time we were preparing a steak supper for the family. We had steak and French fries, of course. We cooked the French fries in a deep fryer. When we put the potatoes in the grease, it bubbled over as grease will do when it's really hot. It went down to the burner, and it caught fire. That pot of grease flamed up several feet high, and we were running around, looking at each other and saying, "What are we going to do?" Donna, in a very calm, placid way, said, "You can put baking soda on it. That'll put it out." We grabbed the box of Arm & Hammer baking soda and dashed some on the fire, and it immediately put the fire out. We said, "Donna, where in the world did you learn that?" She said, "On television." So there is some good that comes from television with children.

Before I left Griffin, I had an idea to write a book on the child's voice. I presented the idea to the guys in Nashville, and they liked it. I was suggesting that I make a recording to coincide with the book, which would demonstrate the ideas expressed in the book. They asked for outline material. I decided to title the book *Children Can Learn to Sing*. They accepted the idea, and I began working toward that end. While I was writing the book, I was also being asked to do many festivals in the summer, as guest conductor at summer camps. This happened in a number of states and associations, putting in practice the things expressed in the book. I also saw the need to include pictures, illustrating many of the conducting techniques discussed in the book. Again, I could feel the Lord's hand in all this, while writing about it and seeing it happen in rehearsals with the children before me. This was the biggest help in doing the book.

I also got to know Dr. Bill Reynolds during this time that I was doing recordings for the Music Department of the Baptist Sunday School Board, since he was basically in charge of all music publications, both the literary and the written music.

An interesting thing happened one day that I will always remember as the Lord making connections happen. At Ridgecrest, I bumped into Dr. Reynolds in the Nibble Nook area of the campus. At about the same time, Dr. Kenneth Hartley came walking up. Bill Reynolds introduced us to each other. We talked for a little bit about music in the church and so forth. This *was* Music Week at Ridgecrest, anyway. Bill left to go to a class he was teaching. Ken Hartley and I carried the conversation further. At that time, Dr. Hartley was head of the music department of New Orleans Seminary. I said to him, "You know, I've been to the seminary, but I have felt the need to complete my undergraduate work before I get any older, if I could." We talked about that for a while. He said, "Charles, I'm not in a position right now to help you, but if I ever am—if I could be of help in your getting that degree, I would love to help you." He said some nice things about my work because he knew about my working with children. He did not know that I was considering writing a book based on that subject. He knew of a lot of other things where my name had come across his desk in publications.

As time went on, perhaps several years passed, I got a call from Dr. Reynolds. We had kept in touch with each other through the years, not like close buddies, but we knew each other well. He said, "Charles, have you ever considered leaving First Baptist, Griffin to go to another church?" I said, "I have had some invitations, but I've turned them down. What do you have in mind?" He said, "I am an interim, part-time minister of music at Immanuel Baptist Church in Nashville, and they are looking for their first full-time minister of music. I would like to recommend you for that position, but I thought I would call you first and see how you felt about it. If you did not want to move from Griffin, I would understand, and there's no need in my mentioning your name to the people at Immanuel Baptist." I said, "I would consider this if there would be some way I could work on my degree and be able to have a church job that would pay me enough to support my family. I think I remember that Belmont College is in Nashville. If I remember correctly, this is a Baptist school, and I think I would strongly consider moving to Nashville if I could possibly go to Belmont and finish my undergraduate degree." He said, "Well, you need to talk to Dr. Kenneth Hartley. Ken is head of the music department at Belmont College. Let me give you his phone number. You call him and talk to him about it." Enough time had passed between the time Bill had introduced me to Ken Hartley at Ridgecrest and the time I was talking to Bill on the phone that he did not really remember having introduced us. I took the number down that he gave me. I went ahead and pretty soon, not immediately, but in a day or so, considered making that call, all the while I was thinking about it and praying about it and discussing it with Mae. I always tried to bring her into the picture on all those kinds of decisions that I made. I put in a call to Dr. Kenneth Hartley. Immediately when we began talking, he said, "Charles, I remember talking with you at Ridgecrest about this, and I was not in a position to help you in any way because I was at New Orleans Seminary and you'd already had seminary training. But I *am* in a position to help you now. I'm head of the music department at Belmont College, and if you decide to come this way, I'll do everything in the world I can to help you do what you want to do and what you need to do with this." I went home and said to Mae, "You won't believe who I've been talking to on the telephone." When she asked "Who?" of course, I said, "Dr. Kenneth Hartley, the man I met at Ridgecrest several years ago. He offered to help me sometime, if he could, to finish my college work. I told him that I enrolled at Furman University in Greenville when I was in a church there and that they would not accept any of my credits from Southern Seminary, which meant I would have to take everything over again if I got a degree from Furman. Not only that, but I would have to take everything in the order that it appears in the catalog, and I would not be able to choose my subjects so that I could take more difficult ones along with easier subjects so I could handle it while working in a church full-time." The way Furman wanted to do it, I would end up with two difficult, heavies together, and I did not want that.

Dr. Hartley said, "That's ridiculous! I've never heard of such!" I told him the registrar said the reason they had that in their policy at Furman was that they do not accept credits from a professional school. I said, "I always did believe they meant by that, like learning to be a barber or beautician, automobile mechanic, or some tech school, and not a school like Southern Seminary." He said, "I'll tell you what. You send me a copy of your transcript, if you can get it, and I'll look at that, and we'll see how many subjects I can accept credit for so you won't have to take them again." I don't know if he was anxious to get a person on campus who had a more mature and valuable experience in church music, but he acted very much like he wanted to help me. I'm sure he did that with everybody else, but it impressed me that he was trying so hard to help me.

The next step was to make a trip to Nashville to talk to Dr. Hartley and Immanuel Baptist Church. When I told Bill Reynolds I was interested in doing this, he went ahead and gave my name to Dr. Gaye McGlothlon, who was the pastor at Immanuel. They had had a part-time minister of music for a number of years, and they wanted to go full-time. When I talked to the pastor, I said, "The only thing is, I had hoped I could have some time to study at Belmont College," and I explained the fact that I did not have a college degree.

I needed to take at least one foreign language to complete my degree. I had had Italian diction at the seminary, French diction, and I sang a good bit of Latin, but because of the association with the German language with music, I felt to take a course in German would be the thing to do. I signed up for it and began my work studying German. It was conversational study and not just grammar. I was learning to speak German pretty well and used it quite a bit when Mae and I went to Germany some years ago, to Oberammergau. Before we finished that two weeks there, the tour guide remarked about how my German had improved.

While I was at Belmont, however, there was a time not too long after I went to school there that I had the need to talk to my German professor. I don't recall what the need was, but there was something I did not understand, and I needed his help to interpret something about the course. I did not know where his office was. As I said, it was only a short time after I went there to go to school. I went to the school office in the administration building and asked where his office was. They said it was Room 404, Hale Hall.

Well, Hale Hall was also the music building. I wondered about that, but they seemed to know what they were talking about, so I went to find Room 404. When I went out of the administration building and started toward Hale Hall, I looked, and there were three floors and a basement. It was not a subterranean basement, but was high enough off the ground that they had windows around it, although part of it was underground. I thought, well, counting the bottom, Room 404 was bound to be on the top floor. So I went in Hale Hall, like I'd been in I don't know how many times. I immediately took the stairway to the left and went up to the next floor, to the next floor, and all the way to the top. I came out in a hallway from the stairway, and I didn't see any 400 numbers.

I walked down the hall a little ways, and I still didn't see it. I could hear water running, like somebody was in a shower, but I didn't dare open a door to find out where in the world 404 was. I went back downstairs to where the music office was and saw my friend Bob Malloy, who was a teacher there at Belmont and director of the male chorus. When I saw him, I said, "I'm trying to find my German professor's office, and they told me that it was in Room 404, and I cannot find 404. Where in the world is it? I went all the way to the top floor, which I figured was the fourth floor, and the numbers up there are still three-something." He said, "You didn't go up there!?" I said, "Yes I did. Why?" He said, "Because that's the girls' dormitory." I said, "You've gotta be kidding!" He said, "No, I'm not. It's a wonder you don't get locked up!" I said, "My word! That would be something! The minister of music at Immanuel Baptist Church is locked up for going in the girls' dormitory!" Well, nothing happened. I didn't see anybody in the hall. I had just turned right around and gone back down and saw him and found out that 404 was in the basement. Now, does that make sense? Every building I've ever seen, you count floors, and the numbers get higher as you go up. But not Belmont! I was kidded about this event when word got around about it.

While I served the church and attended college in Nashville, I was invited numerous times to lead children's choral festivals in various places across the country. The Children's Choir Festival for the state of Oklahoma was held at Oklahoma Baptist University in the city of Shawnee. The festival was two Saturdays, back to back, with about 1,000 children at each festival. As I think about the Oklahoma festival, I'm reminded of something that took place the day before I actually had to be conducting. It happened on the way out there.

I was flying, of course, and the pilot came on the speaker to tell us there was a pretty bad thunderstorm he would have to go through. He was explaining that he'd decided to go around it, and that it might take a little longer to get to our destination, but it would be a much better ride.

The next day, I read in the newspaper there had been a passenger airplane with a couple hundred people on board that crashed as a result of that storm—the very storm I would have gone through had we kept our course. The Lord sure took care of me in all the stuff I tried to do, and I'm so thankful.

All of this work with children was a result of my being asked to record that first cantata, "Lo! A Star!" After that, I was invited to record about another half dozen cantatas and pieces of choral music.

My interest in recording became a hobby, but at the same time, it was very useful in my work. This all began when I was a student at Southern Seminary, and I had the idea of having my accompanist record the accompaniment for the songs I was learning and performing as a voice student. I was able to practice with that tape and have my own private accompanist. This was done because I could not play the piano, and I was not able to have a live accompanist with me all the time. I would take my Silvertone tape recorder from Sears & Roebuck with that accompaniment recording to a practice room on campus. I would sometimes use it at home, too, preparing for recitals and such.

I used a reel-to-reel tape recorder quite a bit throughout my entire music ministry, and it has paid off in many different ways. I bought a nice recorder when I was in Griffin, Georgia, not long after which I was asked to submit that audition recording to Nashville to record "Lo! A Star!" I'm certain that the quality of that tape, being done on the equipment that I had, played a big part in getting that invitation.

On several occasions while we were in Nashville, I was asked to engineer various choral works in Nashville. I would set up the recording equipment in Woodmont Baptist Church, and a group of Belmont College students would come in with their director and record. This was done for the *Youth Musician*.

I recall several cantatas and other albums of music for children. One of these invitations had nothing to do with Baptist work at all, but it was a distinct honor I had to record my children's choir with Holt, Rinehart and Winston publishers in New York. Buryl Red was the editor for that music, and he asked me to train a group of children to do the recording. My children at Immanuel Baptist Church recorded about 15 songs for a public school music series. This was not church music, but it was fun music for children. Buryl brought the sound track on tape and my children recorded with that track in Columbia Studio A on Record Row in Nashville, Tennessee, which was one of the leading recording systems in Nashville. That was quite an experience to do that with those boys and girls.

I tried to be a good father, doing things together with the family, which was difficult at times, because weekends, when the children were out of school, were a busy time for a minister of music. We were able to have some really good times on vacations. I had an idea when we lived in Griffin that I would design and build a camping trailer. I started it in Griffin, and I finished it after we moved to Nashville. It would sleep five people comfortably and had all the pull-out drawers for clothes, food, ice chest, seats to use when eating, etc. All these drawers would also pull out on the outside when we wanted to be outdoors.

The first trip we made using that trailer was to Glorieta, New Mexico for Music Week, during which time I was to teach classes. After that week, we went on to Yellowstone National Park for part of a week. At one point, on our way back toward Nashville from out west, we were camped in a state park. During the late afternoon and evening, we had a really hard rain, maybe even some hail, and strong winds. Our camper was supported by aluminum poles, holding a canvas top. The wind was so bad, we were afraid it would bend those poles, so David and I were on each side of the camper, inside, holding the poles and bracing ourselves against those strong winds. It was frightening to feel how strong that storm was and we didn't know if we were going to make it or not. Mae and Donna were inside with us, of course. Judi was about four or five years old at the time, and was calmly sitting on her little cot in a corner of the camper, looking at a children's book. I looked over at her and said something about not being afraid of the storm, and she looked up and answered, "Daddy, just don't worry 'bout it. God will take care of us." We all looked at one another and remembered that old phrase, "out of the mouths of babes..." We pulled that trailer all over the country and had a good time using it. Remember...no brag, just facts!

The many opportunities I had both in Griffin and Nashville to continue my education and build on my interest in the child's voice and in sound recordings served to strengthen my training and help me to have a stronger church music ministry. I not only received my undergraduate degree, but I experienced many wonderful things in choral music. It is interesting to look back and see how the Lord put so many good things—and people—in place at just the right time, to guide me in what He wanted me to do for Him.

Lo! A Star was the first recorded Junior Choir Christmas cantata for the Baptist Sunday School Board.

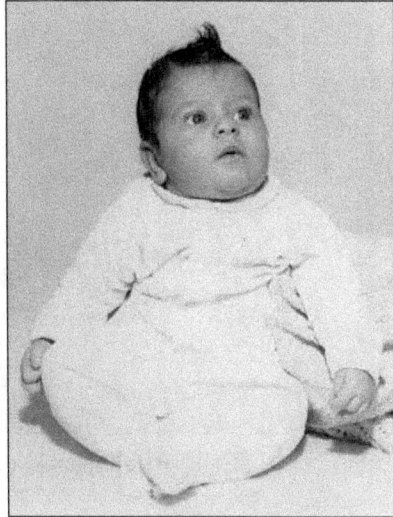

Judith Arlene Crocker was born January 22, 1962

David shot his first deer as a young teen in Griffin, Georgia.

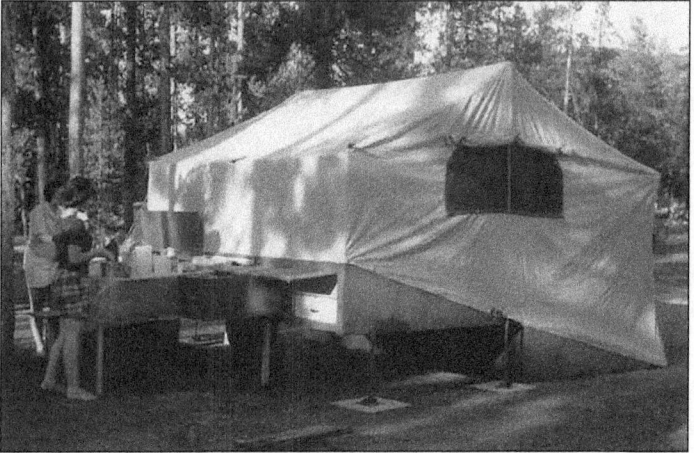

Charles designed and built this camper for his family
to enjoy vacations together.

Charles graduated from Belmont College in Nashville, Tennessee in 1968.

11

Asheville

The writing of my book about the child's voice got put aside while I was in college, trying to finish my undergraduate degree, but most of my invitations to be guest conductor came soon after going to Asheville, North Carolina to become Minister of Music of First Baptist Church. It's kind of interesting that guys at the Sunday School Board Music Department already knew that the Asheville church was interested in me, and I had not heard anything from anybody officially. In fact, that was the first I had heard about it; guys were kidding me, saying, "Oh, I hear you're going to Asheville." I said, "I don't know what you're talking about." They thought I was kidding, but I wasn't. I had not heard a word from Asheville.

When I learned, however, that the pastor of First Baptist in Asheville, Cecil Sherman, had a brother who pastored a church not too far from my church in Nashville, I figured that was how they got word I was going to Asheville. That didn't matter; it just kind of satisfied my curiosity. However, on an early evening in January of 1968, I received a call from Dr. Sherman, asking me if I would talk to them about becoming their minister of music. I was very impressed with the way he addressed the subject and the way he talked to me. I said, "I will consider it, but you need to know one thing." I told him about wanting to finish my college work before I moved. I said, "This is something I've wanted to do for years. I have felt the need for it, and I would be glad to talk with you after I finish." This was in January, and I had already learned I could go to summer school that following summer of '68 and probably work things so I could finish my degree. He immediately said, "Suppose we don't touch you until you finish?" I said, "In that case, I'll be happy to talk with you." He immediately said, "We are making plans to build a children's building in our church, and I'm coming to Nashville with a committee that is responsible for seeing this project through. We are coming there to talk with some guys in the architecture department." The Sunday School Board had all kinds of consultants for most anything about a church, and certainly building a building was one of them. They were not preparing the working drawings, but serving in a consulting, advisory capacity. He said, "Do you think we could arrange to meet you in a nice restaurant and have dinner with you and your wife, with no commitment to anything except to talk?" I said, "I'll be glad to." But when I hung up the phone, I told Mae, "I've never been so impressed talking to a person on the phone as I was then." She said, "Who was it?" I told her, and I said, "They're going to be coming to Nashville, and they want us to meet them at a restaurant." I recommended the Town House, which was a lovely place to eat.

When we met in the restaurant, I was even more impressed with the pastor, and the committee was very congenial also. We had a delightful meal, and we were in a position in the restaurant that we could feel free to talk. We must have talked about an hour or more. I was even more interested, but I kept thinking all the while we were talking, if I do this, I'll probably never get my college degree, and that's something I want to do. However, at that time, we didn't talk much about that. We talked more about the church, what they would expect of a minister of music, and what I would expect from them. Nothing was mentioned about salary, but we discussed all the things necessary to help you decide whether you want to talk further. Mae was impressed with the way the guys talked. It was kind of interesting that Wayne Kinser was on that committee, and as soon as he laid eyes on Mae, he said, "He's hired!"

The committee had a chance to talk among themselves on their trip back to Asheville. A day or so after that, I received a call from Cecil that they wanted to talk further. He said, "How could we arrange another meeting for you to have a chance to meet the rest of the staff and more of the committee?" I said, "Well, it so happens that in about a week, I am to go to Kings Mountain for my father's wedding." I explained that my mother had died on February 7th of 1967, and that my father was remarrying a person from King's Mountain. I would be flying into Charlotte, but I learned I would have a nice layover of about two hours in Asheville. There again, I am convinced the Lord worked this out.

So, I got on the plane to go to the wedding. When it landed in Asheville, I was met by Cecil Sherman, Henry Finch, and Alden Angline. They were three of the staff members at that time. It was kind of interesting that really, the committee to seek out a minister of music was made up of staff members. I told them how unusual that was; that I had never gone about talking to a church in the past that had that kind of a set-up. Cecil said, "Well, we look at it this way. You're going to have to rub shoulders with these guys in making our church go, and if you can't work with them, you can't work with anybody." So they helped decide on the person to fill any position.

I flew on to Charlotte. My oldest brother, Earl, lived in Charlotte, and he met me at the airport and took me to King's Mountain for the wedding. After the wedding, I went back to Charlotte and spent the night at Earl's house. The next day, I flew back to Nashville. I didn't have a chance to talk to Daddy much, of course, with what was happening in his life that night in King's Mountain, but I told him in just a few sentences that I was talking to First Baptist Church, Asheville, and it looked like maybe they were going to want me to become their minister of music. He was happy as a lark. He was happy at getting a good woman in a marriage, but he was also happy that it might work out for me to be only 115 miles from Rock Hill.

After I was back at home for a day or so, Cecil called me again, and said the staff was impressed with me and wanted to know if I would talk further. I said, "Yes, I would, but I need to remind you that I am trying to finish my undergraduate degree at Belmont College, and if I break from this now and move to Asheville, I'll be leaving without my degree. I don't finish my degree until the end of the summer. By taking a few courses in the summer, I can complete my degree and I could come at that time." He said, "We will work with you on that. That's not all that long a period of time." By this time, it was late February, and we were closer to when I would finish college. Things were beginning to move, and Cecil wanted to know if I could come to Asheville to meet the deacons and some people pertaining to the music ministry. I said, "I have done a record album as a memorial to my mother. I have those records on hand now, and I am planning to come through there in about a week to take some of them to Rock Hill." I told Cecil about the album and explained that I wanted to get them to some places I'd served before; since it was a memorial album, I wanted very much for it to sell. I made it clear that all the proceeds from this would go to Connie Maxwell's Children's Home, which was a children's home in South Carolina. My mother was very interested in that home and doing things for them, so I was sending all the money to them to set up a trust fund which could be used to help the children with their college studies. I told Cecil that I only had one request: I wanted a chance to work with the choir on that night, and I asked if he thought he could get the choir there to rehearse with me. It wasn't to be a rehearsal for some performance I was conducting, but it would give me a chance to see what the choir sounded like, and it would give them a chance to see me and the kind of sound I would want from the choir.

Mae and I were driving, not flying, and we stopped in Asheville for that Monday night. I had a chance to work with the choir. Again, the Lord was working in this, in that one of the pieces I rehearsed with the choir happened to be a cantata *On the Passion of Christ* by David H. Williams, an English composer. I was working on the same cantata to be done by my choir in Nashville. I treated the choir rehearsing that night as if they were already my choir. I did this work in Griffin, Georgia, and an ensemble I put together did it at a state music meeting, so I knew the work pretty well. I enjoyed working with the choir on it. Wilda Bell was holding things together with the adult choir during the interim. She had degrees from Mars Hill College and Furman, and she was a public school music teacher at that time. She came to me during a reception they had so I could mix and mingle with the deacons a little and give them a chance to meet me. She said, "Is there any way that you could come back through here on this Thursday night, and conduct this cantata as a part of our Maundy Thursday service?" She was working on it for it to be done for that service. I said, "I think I can. We'll be going back toward Nashville at that time, and it would be a pleasure to stop and conduct the work." It's amazing how things fall into place when the Lord is leading, if we just follow His leadership.

We came back to Asheville, went through that service, and had a good time afterward meeting a lot of people in the church. They wanted to talk further. We had one more meeting with the committee, which happened on the top floor of the Northwestern Bank building. Dr. Joe Frank Hamilton was chairman of the deacons at that time. He was in that lovely dinner meeting we had, and talking with him and the pastor, I said, "The reason I want to be really sure that this is the church I want to come to, and for you to be really sure as a church that I'm the man you want, is that I feel this will be my prime ministry. This is because of my age (I was 36 at that time) and I will have completed more education, and I would be in a position, I think, to move to a place and be able to make it a long tenure." They said, "Now, that really sounds good to us!" I said, "Well, we'll talk further and see how the Lord leads."

A few days after that, I got another call from Cecil saying the choir and the committee and the deacons wanted me, and would I come. I said, "Well, I need to think about this, because I still have this obstacle of finishing my degree in the way." He said, "We wondered if it would be possible for you to come on in early June and commute back and forth to Nashville." I said, "I will look into that with regards to plane schedules." He said they would fly me back and forth, and that I could look into the plane and school schedule to see if this would be possible. After I investigated all that, I called Cecil and said, "For me to move to Asheville in early June, and actually live in Asheville, and have to depend on being in a college dorm during the week so I could be your minister of music would be extremely hard for me to do." He said, "Well, I'll tell you what. Why don't you live at home during the week, which would be much easier on you, and commute to Asheville on weekends?" I said, "Well, now that sounds better after all." That's what we did. Again, every time I came up with a problem, it was solved. I said to myself, "Surely the Lord is in this and wants me to go to Asheville." I prayed about it, we talked about it, and I said to Mae, "It seems the plan he's talking about would work, and it would be a lot easier on you and me and everybody concerned."

I called Cecil early on that Sunday morning because I didn't think it was fair to the choir to keep them hanging on this. I told him and that he could go ahead and tell them I would come to be their minister of music. He said, "That's the best news I've heard in a long time!" This was probably because they had looked and looked for a minister of music and just now felt like they had found one. The first Sunday in June 1968, I appeared in the service at First Baptist, Asheville for the first time for a regular morning service (since I had already been there on Maundy Thursday to conduct the cantata). So, I accepted the call and the pastor's secretary even worked out the travel and bought all the tickets and had them sent to me to fly to Asheville and back. It was set up for me to come Friday after class, and I would have rehearsal on Friday night (can you believe that?). I would stay through the morning service on Sunday, and fly back to Nashville. Saturday was spent trying to find a place to live. That went on for probably half the summer before I finally found a place

I thought Mae would like. I would arrange for her to come with me one weekend it to see it.

Everything was working fine so far as the arrangements with the church, my transportation, and all that, but I ran into another hurdle I had to get over with the school. The registrar at Belmont was having seniors come in to check transcripts with the school catalog, making sure that all the requirements were met. He got in touch with me and wanted me to come in and look at my transcript, compared to the catalog, which I did. Looking at it, he said, "You're going to have to have three subjects in summer school if you plan to graduate in August." I said, "Well, will that be a problem?" He said, "It might be. I think you'll have to get permission from the academic dean before you can take more than two subjects in summer school." The reason for that was that more study was covered in a shorter period of time, and there weren't enough hours in the day sometimes. He said, "If Dr. Schatz (who was the dean) okays it, we'll go ahead and work it out."

So I went straight to Dr. Schatz, told him what had happened with Asheville First Baptist and that I'd already accepted the position to become their minister of music, and would he approve my taking three subjects in summer school to complete my degree." He said, "I'm sorry, Mr. Crocker, but that goes against the rules we have, and if I do it for you, I'm going to be flooded with that sort of thing with other students, and I'll have to say no to them." I said, "Isn't there some way we can do this?" He said, "I don't see how you can. You will have to have these required subjects to get your degree." It was not a matter of my taking an elective; I had some required subjects still to take. I told him that I had waived a certain number of subjects, transferring credits from Southern Seminary to Belmont (you remember this was something Furman would not do). The dean of the music school, Dr. Kenneth Hartley, had done that for me. I don't know about now, but in those days, college would not accept in a transfer a D grade in a subject; it had to be a C or above usually. I had taken a required course at seminary in History, and there was a similar subject in the required subjects I needed in order to graduate at Belmont. I said, "Would it be possible to work this, if you could accept that D for a transfer, and that would give me enough requirements to graduate?" He said, "You go talk to Dr. Hartley. If he okays it, we'll do it."

I knew I had it made then! I went to Ken Hartley and told him what was taking place, and he signed the slip immediately. I went back to Dr. Schatz and handed him the paper Ken had signed. He looked at me and said, "I figured there was some way we could work this." I said, "I sure do appreciate it!" So this meant I didn't have to take the third course, and that made it a lot easier on me. Again, the Lord knew more about required subjects and so forth anyway.

So I enrolled in summer school and started working my plan to finish the studies and graduate and move to Asheville. I met all the requirements at school and at the church, and I looked forward to walking across the stage and receiving that diploma. The formal graduation ceremony had already taken place by this time, and I had to wait until June of '69 to get my diploma. By this time, I was saying "I know more about "have faith in God, he's on His throne" which is part of a hymn I've sung many times.

I commuted the entire summer, back and forth to Asheville. I was able to catch a non-stop flight from Nashville to Asheville on Friday following my last class. People took turns meeting me at the airport, taking me into town. My lodging was at the Blue Ridge Motor Lodge on Tunnel Road. The church furnished me with a car to drive. In those days, instead of having a church bus, they had a couple of station wagon-type vehicles. That gave me the means to drive around town as I needed to, especially getting to church on Sunday morning. Different nice people in the church took turns getting me back to the airport after the morning service. My flight did not leave Asheville until about mid-afternoon.

I remember when I first started doing this commute, Dr. Jess Chapman agreed to be responsible for getting me back to the airport. He told me that he was going to call his wife and tell her he was bringing me to their home for Sunday dinner. I said, "Are you sure you want to do this?" He said, "Oh yes, I think it will be fine." I said, "Well, if it's all right with her, it suits me fine. I'd rather eat a good, home-cooked meal than go to a restaurant anyway." So we went to the airport via his house for lunch. When I got there, I realized that his wife, Frances, had not planned on a guest for dinner and she was apologizing for not having a nice meal on the table. Of course I told her I understood and didn't expect that. She said, "I changed what I was going to have. I was going to have chicken and dumplings, but you wouldn't like that, would you?" I said, "Are you kidding me? Chicken and dumplings is one of my favorite meals!" She said, "Oh, then you would like some?" I said, "Absolutely! Please! That would be wonderful!" I'll never forget how good they were. She was a very good cook, and I enjoyed the meal and the fellowship with them, getting to know them a little better. She remembered my liking the chicken and dumplings when we moved to Asheville and were getting settled in our house. She brought a big pot of if for a meal, and it turned out to be enough for a couple of meals. They were just as good as the first ones I had. I think she thought because I was a minister of music that I would only like gourmet food, but that is not so.

Dr. Chapman took me back to the airport that afternoon, and I flew back to Nashville. Mae would meet me at the airport in Nashville and take me home. This arrangement worked out much better than the first one we worked out with my staying in the dorm during the week. There ain't no place like home, anyway!

As we were approaching the time in August, after I completed my studies, to move to Asheville, I was able to sell our house there on Cheekwood Road in Nashville without any trouble at all. In fact, a friend of mine in the music department at the Sunday School Board bought it. With that in mind, it freed me up to get serious about finding a house in Asheville. Fenton Erwin, a church member there and a realtor, would take me around on Saturday mornings, looking for a house. He hauled me all over Buncombe County trying to find a suitable place to live. I remember walking out on the little balcony outside my room at the motel and looking up the valley. In those days there was a farm house close to the little churches on Chunn's Cove Road. I could hear roosters crowing, see horses running around the pasture, and it just seemed quiet and peaceful. I said, "You know, I wish I could find a house in Chunn's Cove." Well, we did. I came to the house where we live now, 12 Chunn's View Drive. It had everything we needed and wanted in a house, with a few little changes in décor, and we bought it. Mae came with me the next weekend, and I was able to show her the house. It was new; we would be the first people to live in it so there was no problem about seeing it. She liked the house, so here we are. We have lived in this house for 42 years.

I hit the ground running in my church job at First Baptist. I realized after working with the choir and hearing them talk, and after hearing the staff talk, that they were anxious to continue doing good music, which was right down my alley. The choir surprised us with a housewarming, with everything you could imagine given in gifts to get started both in the way of food and other items that were very useful. This made for a really good beginning here at this church.

When we were here only a few weeks, I put together a music program using anthems they already had in the library, and arranged them into what I call a chronology of church music, starting with music of the Renaissance, then baroque, then classical, then romantic eras. I said I could think of no better way to get started with a choir than to work on a concert and present it to the church. This worked out really well.

I mentioned earlier that in talking with Joe Frank Hamilton and Dr. Sherman at a dinner meeting that I thought this would be my "prime ministry." Having just completed more education, and, at my age, I should be able to be the minister of music here for quite some time. When I mentioned "prime ministry," I said, "In fact, you could just call me the Prime Minister of North Carolina!" Not knowing little ears were hearing that, our daughter Judi was with Mae and me, and she heard this statement. It so happened that during the summer when I was commuting, Judi spent some time with her Granddaddy in Rock Hill. I was able to get her to Rock Hill to stay with Dad for a week or so, and when I went to pick her up, my dad said, "I've got a question for you. What in the world is Judi talking about that you're Prime Minister of North Carolina?" I said, "What!?" He said, "She said you were Prime Minister of North Carolina! I asked her what she meant by that, and she said, 'I don't know, but if my daddy says he's Prime Minister of North Carolina, that's what he is!'" I said, "Oh! I remember talking with the chairman of the deacons and the pastor about coming to Asheville, and I said that it would probably be my prime ministry and why it would be, and that it would be a long tenure. That's when I said I could be called the Prime Minister of North Carolina, so that's where she picked that up." I thought that was kind of funny.

This prediction came true. I was Minister of Music here in Asheville for 29 years, and I retired at age 65. People were nice enough to want me to stay on, but I said in talking to the deacons, that if I had reached retirement age not having been here more than just a few years, I would work longer. But at age 65, having been here 29 years, I thought it was time for me to step aside and let someone else come and take over the music. I said, "You must know that I will miss it tremendously" and that's turned out to be true. At the time I'm writing this biography, it has been 15 years since I retired.

A lot of things happened in those 29 years. Some funny things, some that were difficult, including health issues, but I want to stay with the funny things, for a while anyway.

I remember one time on a Sunday morning, when I was leading a hymn, it happened to be *To God Be the Glory*, a hymn the congregation really enjoyed singing. I was leading the hymn in such a way as to show the congregation that I was expecting them to let go and enjoy it. About halfway through that hymn, a blob of plaster fell from the center of the dome ceiling down into the congregation. It so happened that it hit the chandelier and disintegrated to a certain extent, but there were still pieces large enough that, even though no one got hurt, it was very frightening and very unpleasant. I stopped the hymn immediately, and I looked up and said, "Well, I always did want to bring the house down with a hymn, and now I've done it, so let's continue singing." I suggested that the people in that area of the congregation move aside if they felt more comfortable doing so.

There's another funny story that I don't want to forget to mention. We had an organist for a while named Dan Hardin. He did a lot of practicing at the organ during the week. He was a good organist and enjoyed doing great music. He was practicing one day, and I was back in my office. He came running in and said, "Something has happened to the organ!" I said, "What do you mean, is it not playing at all?" He said, "Yes, but it sounds awful! I left the organ to go to the chapel to teach a piano lesson, and it was fine. It sounds like somebody's just gotten up in the pipes and walked around, it is so badly out of tune! I can't imagine what has happened!" I said, "Well, let's go out and take a look and listen, and see what we can come up with."

When we walked out into the sanctuary, standing in the edge of the choir loft, I heard a kind of whistling type of noise. I looked up and a pigeon flew out from where the exposed organ pipes were, flew into the sanctuary, and lit on the chandelier. I said, "Oh, I see what it is!" Dan said, "What is it?" I said, "A pigeon has gotten up there on those tuning sleeves of the organ pipes, and they are very sensitive. He's knocked this organ dreadfully out of tune." The tuning sleeve is right on the end of an organ pipe, and you could take a pencil and knock that thing out of tune if you wanted to. He said, "What in the world are we going to do?" He said it with that high-pitched voice of his. I said, "I don't know but one thing to do." He said, "What?" I said, "I've got to go home and get my rifle and kill that pigeon." He said, "You can't be serious!" I said, "I've never been more serious in my life. What would you suggest? You can stand here and shoo that pigeon all day long, and it's not going to leave this building." The pigeon was flying to the chandelier, then he would fly over to where the cove lights were, then he'd come down toward the organ. There wasn't but one thing to do and that was to kill that bird.

So I came home and got one of my rifles with a very low powered cartridge. I went back to the church and took dead aim. By that time, the pigeon had perched where the television lights would shine through. I dropped the bird, but he fell down behind the ceiling, and I guess his bones are still there. So with that I became known as the "pigeon exterminator."

Almost the same thing happened much later, when John Hewitt was our pastor. He asked "What can we do to get the bird out of there?" I said, "Well, I've done it before, so I'll do it again." He said, "What's that?" I said, "I'll go get my rifle and shoot him." This was on Sunday morning. I came home, and fortunately, we only live about five minutes from the church. I got the same rifle I used before and took it back to the church. I didn't realize how unusual it looked when I was walking from the car into the church on a Sunday morning with a rifle in my hand. People didn't know whether I was going to shoot the pastor or the chairman of the deacons or shoot myself. John Hewitt said, "I've heard about this happening before. I've gotta see this!" He came in the sanctuary, and I was just ready to take aim for the bird. It was in the same kind of place where the TV lights were. I said, "Well if you're going to watch, that's okay, but get down behind a pew. I don't want to be accused of killing my pastor!" I don't think what I was shooting would have killed him, but I didn't want to take any chances. I took dead aim from the balcony and dropped that pigeon behind the ceiling on the other side of the sanctuary.

There's another interesting story pertaining to pigeons that happened, and I couldn't believe what I saw. We were having a funeral in the sanctuary, and of course, the front doors were open quite a bit for people attending the service to enter. There had been a wedding a day or so before, with a lot of rice thrown on the bride and groom. Undoubtedly a pigeon was eating that rice and came on up, pecking away at the rice, and he walked into the sanctuary. He flew around a little bit, but he didn't continue. He stayed perched up on the chandelier, fortunately without any droppings. At the end of the service, the family was going out of the sanctuary on the chapel side. That pigeon flew down onto the floor behind the last person in the family and walked out with the family, through the outside door, and flew away. I said, "Well, a pigeon always looked like a dove, and that's a symbol of the Holy Spirit, so maybe that's what it was."

I've got another pigeon story to tell. We were having a lot of trouble with pigeons at the church. We had so many that they were beginning to be a nuisance with the way they were messing up the property, especially the church building. We decided we needed to do something about it. They always turned to me when it came to pigeons because, as I have already said, I had become known as the "pigeon exterminator."

There is a concrete ledge that goes around the sanctuary building, and this made a beautiful roosting place for pigeons to light. In the wintertime, with the afternoon sun, those bricks would get warm, and the pigeons would come there and perch, but it became a real nuisance in the way they were messing up the building.

I went to the sporting goods store and bought some .22 cartridges that were what's called hollow-point. The bullet would flatten out when it hit its target. That was what I needed so it wouldn't damage the brick too much; it would flatten out when it hit the brick—if I missed. Now, that's *if* I missed!

I went into the Sunday School department that's right above the old offices. There was a classroom with a window that would allow me to see that ledge around the sanctuary. I opened the window and took a class lectern stand to prop my rifle on, and when those pigeons would light on that concrete ledge, they didn't stay there long. I dropped them down to the bottom edge of the sanctuary. It seemed kind of cruel, but we had to do something. The bullets were not only hollow-point, but they were the very lowest velocity you could buy in a .22 cartridge to shoot in a rifle. I sat there one afternoon and killed 55 pigeons. You know a pigeon is a lot like a dove. In fact, there are certain species of pigeons that are the same size as a dove, and I had one at one time. I actually tried raising pigeons when I was a boy because I was so fascinated by them. Then, there I was shooting the birds!

I took a grocery bag and gathered up the dead pigeons. I took them to one of the janitors and asked him if he wanted them. He said he did. He took them home and had a feast on them. I think that the meat would taste a lot like a dove, but I didn't eat any of them.

I mentioned the bird I had, that was about the size of a dove, when I was trying to raise homing pigeons. I had a cousin named Eston Crocker who raised pigeons and raced them. He worked for the post office and the railroad. They would have pigeons shipped to Atlanta and turned loose at a certain time, by railroad time. The pigeon that got back home first, its owner won the prize. There were a number of people in those days raising pigeons for that reason.

Eston was also raising them as homing pigeons for the government, and they were actually used in World War II. They had a leg band with a little pocket on it, and you could put a brief message in it, turn the bird loose, and it would go back home. I got four pigeons from Eston, but I never had any luck much raising them. They would get up to a certain size on the nest, about ready to fly off the nest. There was some kind of disease they had that would wipe them out.

Eston sent me a pigeon that was about the size of a dove, and was one of his fine birds, but she was old. He thought that might help me get started raising pigeons. He sent the bird to me by railroad, in a cage, and he sent a letter to me saying he'd sent it. He told me that I should never let that bird out because it was an old bird, and she would come just as straight back to Spartanburg, where he lived, as she could go. This was strictly a bird for breeding and not for pigeon racing.

I had built a pen that would keep the pigeons in, with a wire top so they couldn't fly out up above. I had put a wire door in it so that when I got ready to train the pigeons, they could fly out and back in just like Eston's had done. He would open the gate on the pen, and the pigeon would fly down, right into the pen where it belonged. The sad part of the story is that I failed one day to close that wire door to the pen, and I got back to the house, looked around, and that old bird was sitting in such a way that I knew she was getting ready to fly out of that gate and head toward Spartanburg. I tried to sneak back to the gate to close it, but I didn't quite make it, and she flew right out of that gate. But it was the most beautiful sight I think I've ever seen. She made some altitude, and she flew in a great big circle, around and around. She got higher and higher and higher. She got so high in that circle that I could hardly see her. If I'd not had my eyes right on her, I would never have known she was up there. She was getting her bearings, and she turned and flew just as straight westward toward Spartanburg as she could go.

I wrote Eston a note and told him what happened. I said I was wondering if she made it back. He sent me a reply and said she didn't make it. Obviously the bird was too old and could not fly that far. Once pigeons started flying toward home, they didn't stop. Shortly after that, I gave up the pigeon business.

Here's another good story on the pastor, Cecil Sherman, I must share.

Many years later, after the pigeon incidents I've just told, Walter Coleman was our minister of education. It was Cecil's day off, and he was in the yard puttering around like he enjoyed doing at the parsonage down Charlotte Street. Walter had to talk to Cecil about something, and he drove down to get with him. Cecil said, "I'm going to keep working in the yard. You just talk, and I'll listen." Cecil was in the process of moving some azalea bushes that had volunteered themselves in certain places in the yard. He was moving those to where he would rather have them and let them grow up and bloom. So he was in the process of doing that, and he said to Walter, "You know, you would think the Lord would have better aim than this!" Almost immediately, a bird was flying over and turned some body waste loose, and it fell and hit Dr. Sherman on the face, right beside his nose! While he was reaching for a handkerchief, Walter Coleman asked, "How's that for aim, Pastor?" Cecil said, "Damn!" That actually happened. I was not there and not a part of it, but I have laughed about that as much as anybody. I saw Walter Coleman not too long ago and asked him again if that was really true. He said it absolutely was.

I took a lot of trips with choirs, especially children's choirs. For fun, we had choir camps for a week in the assembly grounds around the Asheville area, and missions kinds of tours with the youth choirs. We had choir retreats with the adult choir and the concert choir and a youth choir too. These retreats would be in Gatlinburg, and we'd just have a ball for the whole weekend.

One of the mission trips that I tried to take was to southern Texas, in the Brownsville, Texas area, which isn't but just a stone's throw from the Rio Grande River. We were going to work with the many Latinos that worked in that area doing music missions. We planned to sing programs at night at one of the churches and work at getting a crowd in to hear us. However, just a day or two before time for us to go to Brownsville, we got reports on the news that horses in that area were dying with Venezuelan encephalitis. Although it wasn't humans dying, I was really concerned about taking the youth choir down there. I called the health authorities and asked them to advise me. They said, "Don't go down there. We don't know that the horses would be contagious to your choir, but it's too big a risk."

So, in about a week's time, we had completely changed our trip to go to south Miami and work with the migrant workers. This turned out to be a good thing to do. There was a mission, a Baptist church there in the Miami area, that had a minister of music that had gone to Southern Seminary and was a classmate of mine. He pitched in and helped us find a place to stay in a motel and made arrangements for us to go to that church, a Spanish speaking church, and witness through music.

During the time we were preparing to go to Miami, I had to take the music we had planned to do and have it translated into Spanish. We did not sing in Spanish, but we had the text of all the music we did in the hands of the congregation so they could know what we were singing. I was able to find a couple of Cuban people here in town who helped with all that translating. The hotel where we were to stay turned out to be not a good place. It was very scary; we saw blood everywhere, no place to eat except in the bar. The adults got together and said, "We're going to have to move somewhere else and not stay here." What do you do with about 35 or 40 people needing a place to stay on that night? I said, "I know what we'll do. I will call Glenn Wilcox and get him to help me with this." (Glenn owned a travel agency in Asheville that did business all across the world.) I had two of his children with us on the trip. I called him and told him what had happened and that we needed to move. In about thirty minutes' time, he had arranged for us to go to a nice place right on the beach there in Miami, a motel with a nice swimming pool for the kids to enjoy and a good, clean restaurant. We got on that bus in a hurry and went to that motel. Being there instead of the other place added a lot of joy to what we were trying to do down there. We were just about as close to where we would go each night to sing as we would have been at the other place. We would have recreation in the afternoons, and go swimming, etc., but we came out of the pool in plenty of time to get dinner before we would go to the church to sing.

When we were in the pool, I was serving as somewhat of a lifeguard, watching the kids and making sure they were safe. They decided they were going to dunk me in the pool. They were going to throw me in. Instead, I jumped in, and they came in behind me and were going to dunk me under. They tried and they tried, and I got over to the stairway that goes in and out of the pool, and the handrail came down far enough for me to get my right arm locked around it. They never could break it loose to dunk me. I said to Jim Wayne, who was my roommate down there and happened to be the youth director and assistant pastor at our church, "I've got to do something to get them back. I think I know what I'm going to do. I'm going to pretend that my holding onto that stair rail coming out of the pool has ruined my conducting arm." We went to the first aid kit and pulled out a sling. When we went to dinner there in the dining room, I had my conducting arm in a sling. Those kids saw that, and they said, "What happened?" I said, "Aw, it's okay." I didn't act like it was anything much. They said, "What did you do?" I said, "Well, you know when you were trying to break me loose from the pool stair rail, I strained my arm. I'm not going to be able to use it tonight to conduct. I'm going to have to conduct with my left hand only." They acted like they were really sorry for what had happened. They got me anything I wanted for dinner, kept my coffee poured, and all the while they were apologizing very strongly that this had taken place. I said, "Oh, it was all in fun. Don't worry about it."

There was nothing wrong with my arm; I was faking it all the way. We got to the church (we had taken risers with us and they were already at the church), and I said, "Now, you're going to have to get on the risers. I've got to see if I can conduct with just my left arm and hand." They hopped on those risers like they'd never done before, ready to sing. The accompanist was one of the youth, and she began playing one of the songs we were going to sing that night. I started out conducting with my left hand. I purposely made it seem really awkward, and after about a minute or two of that, I said, "I just don't believe I'm going to be able to do this." I pulled my right arm out of the sling, yanked the sling off, and started conducting like I always conducted. Not only where all the kids about ready to kill me, but some of the adults were too.

After the warm-up practice, we went in to the service and had a good time of fellowship and singing for those lovely people. They were so appreciative of what we were doing, and they put together their best Cuban kinds of recipes on one of the nights and fed us like you wouldn't believe.

Another trip we made to Miami after that, we were going to sing in coffee houses. During those days in the early 70's there were coffee houses where young people could go and have fellowship in supposedly a good, clean environment. On the way through Atlanta, we began noticing smoke coming from the right rear of the bus, and it seemed to be a tire. One of the dual wheels on the back of the bus was just about to catch fire it was so hot. The tire was flat, and that made it hit the pavement in such a way that the friction caused it to almost blaze up. We drove slowly off to a cafeteria there in the edge of town and while we were eating, they called the proper people to come change that tire. Then we were on our way.

We made our way on down onto the Sunshine Parkway in Florida, and because I was sitting up in the front seat, opposite the driver of the bus, I could feel a high place on the right front tire, a little bulge or bump. I had had those before on cars, and I knew what it was. I mentioned it to the driver. He said, "These are brand new tires; just put them on today." I said, "Well, when we stop for supper, I'll have you roll this thing forward very slowly and let me look." So he did. I couldn't really see anything, but I sure could feel it when we were going down the road.

Well, we went on down the Sunshine Parkway another 40 or 50 miles, and all of a sudden, that right front tire blew out, and it was all that driver could do to hold it. They didn't have power steering in buses in those days, and it was all he could do to hold that bus to keep it from running off an embankment on the side. The bus was going down the shoulder, clipping these little reflector signs off like they were match stems, and when he finally got it stopped, the bus was leaning so far, I thought it was going to fall over, but it didn't, thank the Lord. Jim Wayne hopped out and said, "Where's your jack?" The driver said, "J-j-j-just wait a minute. I've got to get the blood back in my feet and legs. I am scared to death!"

Of course, we couldn't change that tire, not on that kind of a vehicle. We called the right kind of help and they came with a wrecker. They used the wrecker to jack the front end up and they changed the tire. We went on our way. He was doing about 70 miles an hour when that tire blew, and not expecting it, it was very, very scary. The tire that I figured had the knot on it was the one that blew.

We went on to the part of Miami that is named Homestead. We would set up in the different parking lots of these coffee houses, and sing with our sound system and so forth, trying to witness, mix and mingle with young people, many of whom were very lonely and needed a friend.

I mentioned earlier that I did a lot with older children's choirs. I really enjoyed the sounds they made, and it was fun to try to improve that sound. Through all of this I had invitations to premier new music for children, cantatas, etc. Some of this happened before we came to Asheville, and after we came here, I did quite a bit of it, premiering works at Ridgecrest Music Week.

After coming to Asheville, I was invited to take my Chancel Choir, as I called them (my choir for older children), to the Church Music Conference in St. Louis, Missouri. We accepted the invitation, and I worked it out with Wilcox Travel to fly the boys and girls to St. Louis. That idea alone caused a lot of excitement within the choir. It was kind of "big stuff" for them, and for me too.

We got on the plane at the proper time, and we were going to St. Louis by way of Pittsburgh, changing planes to go on to St. Louis. Of course, we had to de-board and get back on a different flight. A funny thing happened. One of our boys was asked by a lady what kind of group it was, and he told her it was a choir. She said, "Is this the first time you have flown?" He said, "No, it's the second time." He was counting the flight to Pittsburgh as one, then from Pittsburgh on to St. Louis as the second flight.

We went on to St. Louis and sang at the conference. We also sang at the church where John Hewitt, who happened to be our pastor at the time, had pastored in St. Louis. It was a Sunday night service, and we sang two or three of our songs during that service. John Hewitt spoke to his former congregation there. The next day we took the choir to Six Flags over Missouri, I think it was. At least it was that kind of amusement park.

Soon after coming to Asheville, we were invited to record *Freedom Song* by Mary Caldwell, a beautiful patriotic cantata that was composed in keeping with our country's bicentennial. That recording was done in the sanctuary at First Baptist, Asheville. They also premiered the work at Ridgecrest. One of our church members worked really hard at getting us an invitation to sing Freedom Song for the President, but that didn't work out.

Another pleasure I had as Minister of Music here in Asheville was saving the church money by using my woodworking interest to build things such as choral risers and cabinets for storing sound equipment. I built a sound booth in the balcony of the sanctuary when we were live on television, for recording and for broadcast. My interest in woodworking made it possible for me to learn when I was a boy in my father's woodworking shop. This became something that would fit right in with my work as Minister of Music—building sets for musical drama, etc.

I also started a concert series in the church, which began after I was having so many concerts being done primarily with our own people and very few invitations from the outside. We were averaging about 15 concerts a year, trying to utilize talent we had in the church. I decided we had enough we could make it a series, and we printed up nice brochures announcing all that was about to take place in the concerts.

Not too many years after we came to Asheville, I was put in charge of the television ministry. Our church, at that time and up until 1984, was live on television with WLOS TV. This was done in addition to my being Minister of Music. We did some interesting things with the TV ministry. We did some specials that included parts of the choir doing cantatas that were converted into TV specials with our own actors and production team. We did taping and filming outdoors. There was a time when I had boys on Seeley's Castle, perched like Roman soldiers, in costume, as part of the story of the birth of Jesus. This was quite an undertaking for our music ministry to make all this happen.

I began early in my ministry with First Baptist, Asheville, recording all of the choral pieces that the choir did, which helped me to listen and hear things that I needed to hear in order to improve the choir. At the same time, it was a fun thing to do. Over the years, I accumulated hundreds of choral pieces on tape, and I decided to do a weekly 30-minute radio program featuring our music ministry here in the Asheville area. I titled the program "Music for Living" which was done with some narration, scriptures, and prayer. It was aired on Sunday morning while people were getting ready to go to church. This was a good thing to get our music ministry out into the public. David Foster, our music assistant and organist, has a good speaking voice and did some of the readings that went along with the music. Also, Margie Kiser White, who was my secretary at the time and a drama expert, wrote many of the scripts to be done with the music. This was a lot of help, but it was still very time consuming.

To coincide with this kind of program in the church, we developed a very nice tape ministry, making our concerts available not only to church members, but to anyone who would like to have one. All of these were on cassette tapes for years, and when the compact disc format was developed, we added CDs to the cassette ministry. More people were doing away with cassette decks anyway, and CDs were more convenient for hearing our concerts.

As I am dictating this autobiography, I am becoming more and more aware of how much I am using the pronoun "I". I'm well aware of the fact that this can be overdone. But if you remember, earlier in these writings, how I mentioned that Walter Brennan in a movie every once in a while would say "no brag; just fact." I say that again. No brag; just fact. I've tried to put into words what God has meant to me in leading me. In most everything I have done, I felt He was leading me to do it, whatever it was.

Coinciding with our television ministry, I did a number of youth musical dramas on Sunday morning so they could be seen on television. The first one of these happened right after I came to Asheville. I had already done the very first youth musical drama that anybody knew about, entitled *Good News*. We had done this musical drama with my youth group in Nashville before coming to Asheville. Our son, David, was in the very first performance of this, which was in the city of Nashville, and the governor ruled it "Good News Day" or something like that. In Asheville, Donna had a solo part in that musical. She was the rebel that had to sing "I'm a rebel, yes I am!" She was disagreeing with Christianity in the story but was won over before it ended.

When we did that first one in Asheville, the pastor, Cecil Sherman, came to me after the service and said, "I want you to do this on Sunday morning." I thought he had lost his mind because I had never done anything quite like this on Sunday morning when the service was more of a sophisticated nature. I said, "Are you kidding?" He said, "I'm as serious as I can be. I would like for the young people to know that what they're doing is just as important as anything else that happens around here, and I would like for it to be on Sunday morning also because it would be on TV, and we'll reach a lot more people with it that way. So I said, "If that's the way you feel about it, it shall be done!"

I got in touch with the group, and during the next rehearsal we arranged a date to do it on a Sunday morning. The fact that it was done by the Youth Choir, it was more widely accepted in that service than it would have been if it had been adults doing it.

I also did a musical by Buryl Red called *It's Cool in the Furnace,* the Bible story of Shadrach, Meshach, and Abednego being thrown in the furnace. We had a prop that we built to look like a furnace, and the kids were in costumes. This was done with children, not youth choir.

We also did *Hello World!* on Sunday morning. A very interesting thing happened as the musical drama had ended, and we were about to sing an invitation hymn. Jim Wayne, who was associate pastor at that time, came to the stage and whispered in Dr. Sherman's ear that we had had a bomb scare. Somebody had called and said there was a bomb in the church that would go off any minute. We had no choice except to vacate the building right at the end of that hard work.

We also did *Life,* and *Tell It Like It Is,* to name a few more, all of which were done on a Sunday morning in addition to evening performances. I enjoyed working with Cecil because he was so creative in doing things that would be very meaningful to our church and the community when we were on television. One of these he called his "Santa Claus sermon." He asked me to get at least part of one of my children's choirs on a riser on one side of the rostrum, and a Mary and Joseph with the baby on the other side. He was dramatizing the fact that we let ourselves be involved in the shopping for Christmas gifts and partying, etc. instead of focusing on the real meaning of Christmas. At a certain cue, we had a man dressed fully in Santa Claus outfit, come in the side door and walk toward the center of the church yelling "Merry Christmas, Ho! Ho! Ho!" He came to a certain point and just froze. Dr. Sherman leaned over to the microphone and said, "Very confusing, isn't it?" The children had sung a Christmas carol, and there was Mary and Joseph with the Babe, and then Santa Claus comes in. This received a lot of attention and comment, not only in our church, but throughout the community.

About once a year, I tried to do a concert myself, as Minister of Music, singing everything from hymns to heavier music from oratorios and cantatas. Fairly soon after we came to Asheville, I decided to do a concert with Carole James. She would sing a certain group of pieces, and then I would sing a group, and then we were going to be combined to sing several duets. This was to be done on a Sunday evening. On the day that we were to sing, a very interesting thing happened. I was in the sanctuary on that afternoon, preparing for the program, setting up microphones and tape recorder, as I did with all the concerts. We did not have a sound booth for recording and broadcasting at that time, therefore, for what recordings we did of concerts, the tape recorder was down front with somebody like Dick Hart, who happened to be good at this kind of thing. He would run the tape recorder. I had bent over to put a tape on the recorder and get it ready, and when I did, something in my back popped. I went to my knees, and I absolutely could not get up. Pat Jewsbury was the accompanist for that program, and she was also my secretary at that time. She happened to be there when this happened. I asked her to call Dr. Chapman to see if he could possibly help me out of this problem. Carole James came in about this time and said, "What are we going to do?" I said, "There's no way I'll be able to sing with you tonight." When I asked Pat to call Dr. Chapman, who was a very faithful choir member in the adult choir, to come help me, he came and brought his cousin or some relative that was visiting with him, and the church had a stretcher. These two men put me on the stretcher, put me in the back of a station wagon, and took me to my house. They helped me in and got me across the bed. To make matters worse, the next day was supposed to be the first day of children's choir camp, which had already been planned, the materials purchased, all the organizing done with adult helpers, etc. I said, "How on earth can I have that choir camp the way I feel right now?" I could not move. Dr. Chapman called one of his orthopedic doctor friends, and he said most likely it was a pulled muscle and not in a joint, so he prescribed Equagesic medicine. This was a three-layered pill that had a pain reliever, tranquilizer, and muscle relaxer all in one pill. When I got those pills and took one, it wasn't long before I started feeling great. Believe it or not, it helped me enough that I was able to go ahead with the choir camp plans.

I believe some of the best work I did as a minister of music was working with our children in choir retreats and camps, when we would go to an assembly like Camp Merri-Mac for almost a week. During this time we learned a lot of classical music. Even though they were children, they seemed to enjoy the classics. Not only did we learn a lot of music, but we also had worship services like "morning watch", as we called it, in an open-air setting. We had etiquette rules at mealtimes; they were built into little songs such as "Put your napkin in your lap, Mr. Crocker! Put your napkin in your lap, Mr. Crocker! (to the tune of *If You're Happy and You Know It*). "We have seen you do it twice, and it isn't very nice! Put your napkin in your lap, Mr. Crocker!" And of course, we learned etiquette at other times also.

The morning hours were spent learning and rehearsing music, and the afternoons were taken up with free time and theory study plus a lot of swimming in the lake. We also had fun giving a trophy to the cabin that was the cleanest every day. This trophy was handmade with two different sizes of tin cans soldered together, the big one on the bottom, the smaller one on the top, with a funnel sticking out of the top and two spoons curved for the handle. The first time we had this, the children named it "Cecil" to honor our pastor, Cecil Sherman. I don't know how honored he was, but he kind of liked it anyway!

Much music was learned during the week and memorized and then performed for the parents and friends on the last night of camp. This music was sung again all during the year in addition to many other pieces.

One year, the children were excited to learn a musical drama, entitled *Come Messiah, Come*. They had not laid eyes on the music or the drama before they arrived at choir camp. Besides learning several classical pieces, the children that year auditioned for drama parts, memorized the lines, learned the music and helped to make costumes for themselves all during that week. They performed the musical for their parents on the Friday evening, and I did not even have to conduct them, because they had memorized everything so well. I ran the tape for the sound track while they sang and acted. The children acted out their parts with emotion and real feeling and did a wonderful job performing. This was the most challenging time my children's choir had ever had, but they rose to the challenge and really outdid themselves.

Another good thing to include here about the tape ministry is the *God Will Take Care of You* recording, which was done with the hope of blessing people in adverse circumstances. In working with our senior adult choir (we called them Forever Young but they're now called the Jubilee Choir), I did musical dramas which amounted to narration along with choral work. This seemed to be the best thing to use in nursing and retirement homes to encourage those in that kind of need. We would learn the music in rehearsals on Tuesday afternoons, and several times during the year, we went to nursing homes to sing these pieces.

One of the pieces we learned that went over really big was *God Will Take Care of You*. The message was very strong to help those who were at this time in their lives. It was based on the old hymn by the same title. As we learned this piece and performed it, I came up with an idea to record my voice singing with the sound track, and to add my daughter Judi's voice as the narrator. I put it on CD, and after having this ministry for several years, I have given many copies of this music to people who are mourning the death of a loved one or some very ill person in the hospital. I was able to get permission from the Music Department in Nashville to use this music in this way. I'm proud to say that it has done a lot for many people. It's had very little to do with my singing, but it was a strong gesture on our part to reach those who are in need.

While I was an active minister of music, I became fascinated by piano tuning. When we had a piano tuner coming in to the church wherever I was, it was fascinating not only because it was pertaining to music, but it was kind of mechanical too. I decided I wanted to learn to tune. After talking to different tuners and watching and listening to the way the sound of the piano changed, I finally bought a few tuning tools and started trying to do it. This happened about 1975, and I have been tuning pianos ever since. I wouldn't take anything for having learned how to do this, because it has served to provide a little extra money along the way. At the same time, it was pertaining music, the mechanics of which I've always been interested in. At the time this story is being written, I am still tuning pianos at 80 years of age. The fact that I have very few opportunities to conduct choral music anymore, this helps me feel I have my hands in church music in some way.

One of the last building programs First Baptist had was a $10 million renovation of the existing building, with some new parts added. This was about 2007 or 2008, about ten years after I retired. Much of the renovation took place in the sanctuary, with new pews, new choir loft chairs, new pulpit furniture, new carpet, and many additions to the sound system for recording, broadcast, and closed-circuit television.

They completely renovated the rehearsal and robing area and incorporated a new space that would be an "auditorium", as they called it, that would serve as a rehearsal room for the choirs. It was also intended to be a good lecture hall, in that it is tiered and easy for people to see the conductor or person speaking in a lecture. There would be a nice sound system in that area, and a small recording studio with a large glass window for viewing what was being recorded. I have used that space several times for serious recordings for the church.

When this auditorium/rehearsal area was finished, they decided to name it the "Charles Crocker Auditorium", with signs all over the church directing people to it. That one thing is probably the biggest honor I have ever had, especially in a very long time. I still can't get accustomed to people saying "we're going to meet in Crocker for rehearsal…" This room has already been used several times for funerals too, as it is conducive for any kind of gathering in a church. On the tiers, it will seat about 150 people.

Another part of that renovation program was to completely re-do the inside of the chapel, and they made it a very nice room for small weddings and funerals, and it's used every Sunday morning for an 8:30 service. Small concerts also take place in that room. The altar area in the chapel is really a Lord's Supper table and two chairs, and above that, was a large, blank wall, that previously, was the front of a stage. They had closed that stage in and this large wall, they decided, needed a cross as it would be related to the Lord's Supper table. They came to me and asked me if I would build a cross to blend in with the furnishings and also match somewhat the one we had in the sanctuary. I enjoyed doing that. I made it out of solid walnut and hung it in such a way that it looks like it's suspended in mid-air. This was done by a very small wire fastened to it, going up into the loft. It's difficult to see the wire.

As I was building that cross, I came to a decision to dedicate it in Mae's honor. There's a beautiful plaque in the back of the chapel with wording as follows:

> *The cross seen above the altar*
> *was built and given by Charles Crocker*
> *in honor of his wife,*
> *Mae Steele Crocker*
> *September 27, 2007*

When I finished it and got it hung, I decided to have just the family gather for a small dedication service. I asked Donna to read scripture pertaining to the cross. Judi sang one stanza of "When I Survey the Wondrous Cross", and David did a dedicatory prayer. I had already done my part when I built the cross. I felt really good about doing that for my church, and also the fact that I included Mae in this dedication. The fact that this is an autobiography for me, I realized that I have not said enough about Mae. Mae has always been a very important part of the things I have done in my life. I wanted to express my love and appreciation for her through all the years of support she had given me while I was Minister of Music.

For the most part, I have had good health all during my life; however, there have been times when things were pretty tough for me in that way. The first instance was in

1989, when I had to have angioplasty surgery on my heart. I became active in exercise, and during that, I learned that I had an artery that was closed up in my heart. When I would ride my bike, after a while, I began to have tightness in my chest. When I stopped riding, it would go away. When I'd go back to riding, it came back. When this happened two or three times close together, I went to the telephone and called my doctor. He put me on a treadmill and immediately sent me to a heart doctor for care. Dr. John Lawrence did angioplasty surgery and put me back in good shape.

In early January 2011, I began having serious trouble with my heart. I had reached the point where I thought I had to do something about it, so I went to my doctor and told him what was going on. Usually, he had so many patients it would take several weeks to get an appointment to see him, however, the Lord took care of the situation in that we'd had a lot of snow the week after Christmas, to the point where the doctor had a lot of cancellations, and they told me to come right on.

When I saw him, I said, "I want to be sure I don't have congestive heart failure." He checked me out with x-ray pictures, listened to my heart, and I went to Mission Hospital from his office that day, in an ambulance. It was a serious case of congestive heart failure and I needed immediate attention. In just a few days' time, I had open-heart surgery, including seven bypasses and two valves in my heart taken care of—one repaired and the other replaced. I also learned I had a hole in my heart that I didn't know I had. Once again, I felt the presence of God with me through all of this. I think he was with the doctors too, because they put me back into pretty good shape. I give God the praise for being able to go about a pretty normal life, and I hope I can continue serving him even though I am now 80 years old.

Mae has been a real blessing to me through all of these health problems, helping me with medications, doctor schedules, and so forth. There was one time I had seven different doctors treating me at the same time; Mae has helped an awful lot in keeping everything straight, and I love her for it. The rest of the family has been wonderful too, showing concern for my condition, helping any way they could, to get me through all this.

Now, looking back, I can still say that the years I served at First Baptist Church in Asheville were my "prime ministry" because it is where I served the longest and had the most fulfilling ministry of church music. The Lord led me through many challenges and many opportunities to serve Him and other people, and through it all there were also many blessings.

Charles completed his book,
Children Can Learn to Sing in Asheville.
Photos were included
to show conducting gestures and
techniques to help directors produce
good choral sounds.

Charles' signature conducting
gesture, symbolizing the open throat
(arched upper hand) and dropped
jaw (lower hand), as well as mouth
formation for a pure vowel sound
-- used in combination to produce a
quality head tone for good singing.

Charles' first recording "studio" at First Baptist, Asheville,
was in a corner of his office, adjacent to the choir room.

The Church Choir and Chancel Choir (older children) singing at Christmas with orchestra at First Baptist, Asheville.

Crocker Auditorium

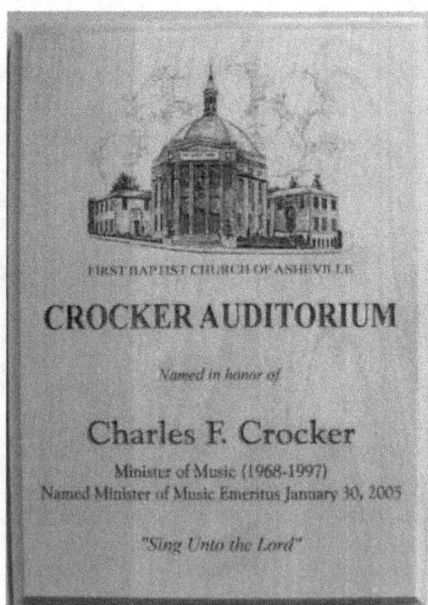

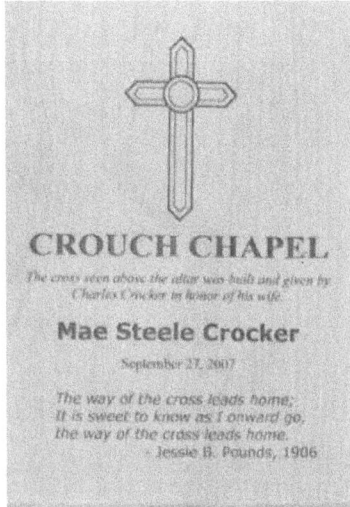

CROUCH CHAPEL

The cross seen above the altar was built and given by
Charles Crocker in honor of his wife.

Mae Steele Crocker

September 27, 2007

The way of the cross leads home;
It is sweet to know as I onward go,
the way of the cross leads home.
- Jessie B. Pounds, 1906

Charles built this cross for the
First Baptist, Asheville, chapel
in honor of Mae.

Charles and Mae, 1993

Crocker's final concert

Charles Crocker, standing, goes over music with organist David Foster at Asheville First Baptist Church. Crocker, retiring minister of music at First Baptist, will conduct his last concert at 7 p.m. Sunday.

Minister of music paid heed to father's words of wisdom

In a feature article in the Asheville Citizen-Times, Charles is recognized near the time of his retirement for 29 years of service to the church and community through his music ministry.

Charles and Mae celebrated 50 golden years of marriage.

Judi, Donna, Charles, Mae, and David in 1999.

12

Special Honors

As the previous chapters followed a chronological sequence of my life story, I think one last chapter is needed to mention some additional, very important parts of the story from various points in my life. Also, because they are special honors, I feel the need to dedicate a separate chapter to them, so their meaning and importance to me is not lost in the middle of the rest of story.

Our three children, David, Donna, and Judi, coming into our lives rounded out a beautiful relationship, and I wouldn't take anything for the honor and privilege I have had in being their father!

David was born early in our marriage. After finishing high school, David decided to become a minister, and he went through four years of college, three years of graduate school at Southern Seminary, getting a master's degree, and later a doctor's degree which equipped him to be the kind of preacher and pastor he wanted to be as far as his education was concerned. It meant a lot to him to do this. He pastored churches for a number of years, after which, he decided he wanted to do something in church work "right where the water hits the wheel," that is, Operation Inasmuch. This is an organization he started when he was at Snyder Memorial

Baptist Church in Fayetteville, North Carolina, but he did not take steps toward making this his full-time service to God and fellow man until after he pastored Central Baptist in Knoxville, Tennessee. Mae and I are very proud of him and what he has done in this regard with his life.

Donna was born two years after David. Donna equipped herself at the University Hospital in Chapel Hill, North Carolina, to become a radiology technician. She has given selflessly to the business of healing and serving people who are hurting. She has developed into being an office manager for an orthopedic business, overseeing the x-ray technicians and handling much of the business affairs of three different offices. Donna has also been active in her church, singing in the choir, along with many other things she does in the church to help keep it alive. Donna and her husband Scott have made Durham, North Carolina their home.

After ten years in our home with only two children with us, Judi was born when we were living in Griffin. Judi is very gifted in music, and has used this gift unselfishly down through the years to the glory of God. For a number of years, Judi served different organizations in the Asheville area in the field of nonprofit fundraising, public relations, and special events. She worked at Givens Estates, a local retirement community under the auspices of the Methodist Church, and she did much to make this organization attractive to retired people who need care. Judi has always had joy in serving the church through her musical talents.

It has been mentioned several times that I was active as a children's choir specialist, not by any desire on my part to become such, but it was the fact that I was able to enjoy working with children in choral settings. You will remember from earlier in my story that as a result of this interest, I did many recordings and other musical materials for directors. All of this brought about many invitations to do state music festivals where children from all over the states would gather in a church or school auditorium, and I would be the guest conductor to work with them. These festivals also benefited the directors, especially the lay-type director who had not had much training but was willing to work with boys and girls. I have done state festivals and camps in North Carolina, South Carolina, Tennessee, Florida, Mississippi, Kentucky, Alabama, Louisiana, Ohio, Maryland, Illinois, Texas, New Mexico, Missouri, Oklahoma, Arkansas, Georgia, and Virginia.

While living in Asheville, I was one of three conductors chosen to serve as guest clinicians for the Church Music Workshop Institute hosted by New Orleans Baptist Seminary. Lloyd Pfautsch and Eric Routley were the other guest clinicians. Seminary students attended this event, and it was open to outside ministers of music too. It ran for nearly a week, so I stayed on campus. There were also chapel services for everyone at the seminary, and I was asked to sing. In the service there were theology, music, religious education, and other students, so it was a real honor to be invited and to be asked to sing something for the chapel service. I sang *Be Thou Faithful unto Death* by Felix Mendelssohn, part of the St. Paul Oratorio.

After the workshops at New Orleans Seminary, I was scheduled to fly straight to Jackson, Mississippi to do a state-wide children's choir festival. It took place at the Jackson Coliseum downtown. I walked into that coliseum, and I looked up at those kids—they filled a good portion of the space—and I said, "How many kids are in this room?" They said they had registered 2,700 children. I got on the platform they had built on the floor level, and the children were on the tiered part of the coliseum. I had a microphone hanging around my neck, and I directed those children. I told people I felt like Cliff Barrows leading the singing in a Billy Graham Crusade.

The way festivals usually worked, there was a morning rehearsal, then a lunch break followed by a dress rehearsal. By evening, the kids performed their concert, doing all the music we had worked on that day. The kids were supposed to have come already knowing the music, but that wasn't usually the case. Sometimes the kids were not as prepared as they should have been, and it meant more work was needed in the rehearsals. With 2,700 children in a large coliseum, that was a big challenge.

The Georgia Choristers Guild invited me to be guest conductor for a four-day camp children's music camp near Toccoa, Georgia. There were 200 children or more from all over Georgia. That camp was one of the most delightful festival experiences I ever had. Those children were sharp as a tack, and it was really a delight to conduct them. We weren't doing easy music either.

This camp went so well that I was later invited to do a festival at St. Phillip's Cathedral in Atlanta, Georgia. The Atlanta Choristers Guild Children's Festival hosted about 450 children, and it was held at the cathedral. A cathedral is shaped like a cross with a long nave from the pulpit or chancel area to the doors, and two side wings. I stood on the platform and directed the children, who filled the cathedral. This was one of the biggest honors I ever had. Close to a dozen excellent musicians from the Atlanta Symphony were in front of me as well. I worked with the children in the morning, had a lunch break, then I directed the children singing in a worship service. What a sound it was! We performed pieces by Bach, Handel, and many other major composers.

I was honored in 1987 to be chosen as one of 20 conductors to conduct at the Oregon Bach Festival. This is a very sophisticated, 17-day festival in Eugene, Oregon. It is held at the university and at the 5,000-seat auditorium in downtown Eugene. Orchestra players and vocal soloists come from all over the world, and they form a choir of about 55 people, who served by doing concerts themselves. But they were also the choir for conductors like me.

When I decided to do this, I learned I had to furnish an audition tape for them to hear a chorus with orchestra which I had prepared, and also a letter of recommendation from some important conductor here in the Asheville area. The Asheville Symphony conductor, Robert Hart Baker, wrote a nice letter of recommendation that was sent to Oregon, and it played a big part in my being chosen to be one of the 20 conductors. We had classes observing Helmuth Rilling, a world renowned choral conductor, working with the 55-voice choir. We would start rehearsing a Bach cantata or some other major work completely cold at 1:15 every afternoon. At 5:15 in the early evening of the same day, we would perform that work. We rehearsed first with piano, we added the soloists with piano, then we rehearsed with the orchestra. I have never felt as intimidated, before or since, as I was in that setting. Each conductor was assigned part of a major work to conduct. Several people were conducting the same thing in rehearsal, and Dr. Rilling and the man in charge of the festival would choose a conductor from those rehearsals to conduct in the performance. I'm really proud to say that every time I conducted in rehearsal, I was asked to conduct in the performance.

Another thing during that festival that kept us on our toes was that the small auditorium where these concerts took place, seating about six or seven hundred people, there would be about 150 to 200 people in the auditorium besides the choir members, the orchestra, and Helmuth Rilling. They were observing Rilling working with the conductors, and we were right there in front of God and everybody. People paid money to hear the concert at 5:15, but they were allowed to be in the auditorium to observe his work with the conductors.

A very interesting thing happened during that time. I was asked to conduct part of those 17 days, and we were doing a Bach cantata. The balcony in the auditorium was built in such a way that the ends of the balcony down toward the stage had a curved stairway that would bring you right down onto the stage. Fortunately, Mae was there to watch me conduct in the rehearsal and also in the performance, and she came down during the little break we had before the performance. She said, "Charles, isn't that Dr. Dahlin over there?" as she described a certain place in the auditorium. I looked and said, "Absolutely." He was my conducting professor at Southern Seminary in addition to other things I studied with him. He's the one who got me on the right track as far as conducting is concerned.

Also, while I was sitting on the stage, waiting to get up and do my rehearsing, I felt a hand on my shoulder from behind, and there was Ferrold Stephens, my voice teacher who also taught me many other things at the seminary. He leaned over and said, "Charlie, show 'em what you can do. After all, you've had good training!" That was kind of a teasing way of taking credit for me, as if he wanted to have credit. So there I was conducting in a performance, with my old conducting teacher and my voice teacher in the audience, neither of whom knew the other one was going to be there! Things like that don't just happen. There's a Power somewhere, and I think I know where, that causes it to happen.

After the performance that day, Mae and I went with each of those men and their wives next door to a nice restaurant. We just had a ball reminiscing about seminary days and talking about music in general.

I was greatly honored many times by the adult choir at First Baptist, Asheville, showered on birthdays with nice gifts. I was really surprised on my 25th anniversary at the church, that the choir had secretly commissioned an anthem to be composed for this occasion. The president of the choir came to me one day and asked what was my favorite hymn. I said, "Well, I have a lot of hymns I like, but if I had to choose one favorite, it would be *My Faith Has Found a Resting Place*." Well, I did not know why he had asked that question, and did not think any more about it.

A few months later when my 25th anniversary was coming up, on behalf of the choir, he had David Schwoebel to compose an anthem based on that hymn tune and text. The thing that really got me was that they'd had secret rehearsals to work on it, and I had no idea it was happening. On the morning of my 25th anniversary celebration, the president of the choir surprised me by conducting the choir singing that anthem. That was my first time to hear it. This was such a nice thing for them to do. The hymn anthem has since been published by Hinshaw Music Company in Chapel Hill. Proper credit pertaining to the honor bestowed on me is found on the front page of music. The entire evening service on that day was given over to a very nice celebration for my 25 years of service with the church.

By the time of my retirement in 1997, I had served First Baptist Church in Asheville for 29 years. This was a thrilling time for me, and filled with many emotions as choir members, church members, and others in the community expressed their appreciation to me for my years of service through music ministry.

On the first Monday in June of that year, at the time of our usual church choir banquet, the choir took the opportunity to make it an appreciation dinner to honor me. In fact, you could call it a "dinner and roast." It all lasted approximately three and a half hours, with many of the choir members coming to the microphone saying nice things to me, expressing their love for me. Some comments were heart-warming, some were funny, some were reminiscent, but all of them were sincere and very special. They also had some guest professional musicians to come sing or play during that time, and these were people who sang or played with me many times when I was conducting. I was honored by the thought and planning that went into that special "roast" which covered 29 years of music ministry.

In addition to the choir's recognition of my retirement, the church held a church-wide reception on Sunday afternoon of my last day as minister of music. Down through the years, the entire time I was Minister of Music, not only at First Baptist Asheville, but in other churches before coming to Asheville, Mae had secretly kept all kinds of documents, including newspaper articles, concert programs, and bulletins, about things I was doing in music in our church or other churches or choral associations. All of these filled 12 large three-ring notebooks. These books were spread out on tables at the reception on my last Sunday so that anyone could see them.

As I mentioned earlier, for many years I kept recordings of all the concerts and many of the other individual pieces of music like Sunday anthems on tape. All of these tapes were recorded on very professional equipment which we had in our church sound booth, and they were carefully filed on reels. Not too many years ago, sound recordings shifted from tape to compact discs, or CDs. Most of the concerts have now been transferred from tape to CD, and anytime I needed information to put on the jewel case booklet for the CD, I would refer to that beautiful set of scrapbooks that Mae put together. I have yet to need information about any concert or anything we had on tape that she didn't have covered in the memorabilia.

Another very meaningful experience for me was to do something with the choir and orchestra that I had always wanted to do. That happened to be Handel's *Messiah* in its entirety. When church choirs do *Messiah* it's not very often you hear of them doing the entire work. For the Christmas season of 1996, my last Christmas choir concert, we did a full performance of this glorious work. We did every note of every chorus. The solos were slightly abbreviated with only some of the repeats deleted, so you had the feeling of hearing the entire solo because of the text.

You remember earlier in this autobiography what Handel's *Messiah* meant to me as a boy, and how I tried to learn parts of it. It was a thrilling experience for me down through the years to conduct portions of Handel's *Messiah* many times, but the most extended performance of it was December 1996.

In addition to having the choir sing the commissioned anthem *My Faith Has Found a Resting Place*, I have requested that the recording of this performance of *Messiah* be played in its entirety at my funeral. It would be carefully explained to the public that it is being played for those who want to hear it, beginning early enough before the service time and ending just before the family would enter the service. Since this is on recording, it can be done very easily through our magnificent sound system in the church, in stereo, so it will sound like the choir and orchestra are right there in person. I can't think of any better way than that for me to be remembered. Of course, I realize I will not be hearing it...or will I? I'll find out someday. This is no attempt to be emotional toward the end of my biography, but I think it's important for people to know about this.

It has been a pleasure for me to serve God as best I could down through the years as a minister of music, fulfilling that call which came to me as a boy when I was talking to my

father who said, "Give your life to Him and he'll not make
a mistake with it." I've tried to do just that as best I could.
I haven't done everything right; there are times I probably
didn't follow his leadership enough, but I have tried to be
the kind of minister of music that he would want me to be.

To God be the glory for any and all good things that may
have been accomplished through my music ministry! Amen.